CRITICAL READING

SAT Study Guide

PASS *YOUR* **SAT**

© 2014 Breely Crush Publishing, LLC

*SAT is a registered trademark of the College Board and its affiliated companies, and does not endorse this book.

971032914143

Published by Breely Crush Publishing, LLC
10808 River Front Parkway
South Jordan, UT 84095
www.breelycrushpublishing.com

ISBN-10: 1-61433-479-X
ISBN-13: 978-1-61433-479-8

Printed and bound in the United States of America.

Table of Contents

Ready to Get Started?

Are you ready to get the best score possible on the reading section of the SAT? This study guide will help you learn new words and strengthen your existing vocabulary. This is one of the easiest and best ways to boost your score on the reading section. You will also practice reading passages, comparing the content and context while answering sample test questions.

Study Plan

One of the first things to do is to set up a study plan. Determine when you will have time available to study. Plan out what you need to do, and place it in time blocks where you will have enough time to accomplish everything you need to do. Keep your studies in segments. Trying to do too much at once will make study more difficult.

Work hard, but if you start becoming too distracted then take a short break. Don't make it too long or you will find it hard to get back into your studying mind set. Try to study in a place that is good for you, comfortable but with few distractions. Studying at the kitchen table might be great when no one is around, but while everyone is in there cleaning up after dinner might not be as good.

Besides trying to study for the upcoming test, make sure that you are still working on your existing classes and are completing your coursework the best you can and on time. Procrastination makes everything seem worse than it really is. Start early so that you don't have to do everything in one night.

Create little goals for yourself, keeping in mind your ultimate goal of passing your test with the score that you want. But, make sure that you are aware of when your deadlines are so that you give yourself enough time to accomplish what you need to.

Don't forget that goals have the following attributes:

- SPECIFIC: Study pages 2-5 in the text today
- MEASURABLE: Does your goal have a way to show your progress?
- CHALLENGING: A stretch outside your comfort zone
- REALISTIC: Something that you can actually complete
- STATED COMPLETION DATE: When will it be accomplished?

Don't forget, a goal not written down is merely a wish.

Vocabulary

VOCABULARY LIST #1

Abasement	humiliation, to bring down or lower, humble
Abstemious	abstinence from or moderation of indulgence
Adulation	praise, devotion, flattery, admiration
Bombast	arrogant or pretentious language
Brusque	rude and abrupt manner
Choleric	hot-tempered, irritable
Clairvoyant	able to see the future, psychic
Desist	to cease or stop doing something
Effusive	unrestrained, overly demonstrative, overflowing
Garrulous	talkative, chatty
Hiatus	pause
Impartial	without preference, unbiased
Inept	incapable, inappropriate, incompetent
Levity	lacking appropriate respect, flippant, joking
Malleable	easily manipulated or shaped
Nefarious	evil, wicked
Obsolete	no longer used, outdated, archaic
Panacea	a cure-all, universal solution
Personable	easily related to, attractive
Poised	good-mannered and dignified, or in balance
Queue	line of people
Robust	full of energy, strong, healthy
Serene	tranquil, calm
Vital	important, necessary, alive, energetic
Vivacious	full of life, animated, energetic

NOW YOU TRY

Match each word from the column on the left, with its definition from the column on the right.

1. Abasement		a. incapable, inappropriate, incompetent
2. Abstemious		b. able to see the future, psychic
3. Adulation		c. line of people
4. Bombast		d. no longer used, outdated, archaic
5. Brusque		e. tranquil, calm
6. Choleric		f. arrogant or pretentious language
7. Clairvoyant		g. humiliation, to bring down or lower, humble
8. Desist		h. full of life, animated, energetic
9. Effusive		i. talkative, chatty
10. Garrulous		j. without preference, unbiased
11. Hiatus		k. easily manipulated or shaped
12. Impartial		l. abstinence from or moderation of indulgence
13. Inept		m. easily related to, attractive
14. Levity		n. important, necessary, alive, energetic
15. Malleable		o. unrestrained, overly demonstrative, overflowing
16. Nefarious		p. a cure-all, universal solution
17. Obsolete		q. rude and abrupt manner
18. Panacea		r. lacking appropriate respect, flippant, joking
19. Personable		s. good-mannered and dignified, or in balance
20. Poised		t. hot-tempered, irritable
21. Queue		u. full of energy, strong, healthy
22. Robust		v. to cease or stop doing something
23. Serene		w. praise, devotion, flattery, admiration
24. Vital		x. pause
25. Vivacious		y. easily manipulated or shaped

ANSWERS

1. g
2. l
3. w
4. f
5. q
6. t
7. b
8. v
9. o
10. i
11. x
12. j
13. a
14. r
15. y
16. k
17. d
18. p
19. m
20. s
21. c
22. u
23. e
24. n
25. h

VOCABULARY LIST #2

Abhor	to hate, detest
Accolade	praise, applause, honor
Arable	suitable for farming or cultivation
Belabor	to explain or work at something more than is necessary
Bristle	short, stiff hairs or stiffening to show irritation
Cerebral	intellectual, knowledgeable
Debility	weakness, disabled, or incapability
Diffident	unconfident, reserved
Enigma	mystery, puzzle, riddle
Exacerbate	worsen
Expedite	speed up
Innocuous	harmless, inoffensive or boring
Kindle	to ignite or excite
Legend	the key to a map or a historical explanation, myth
Malady	illness
Mellow	soft, gentle, sweet (ripe)
Odious	hateful, abhorrent, unpleasant
Palisade	a fence or wall made of posts
Perjury	lying under oath
Posthumous	after death
Quarantine	isolate, often to stop spread of illness
Recluse	a person who isolates themselves from others
Revere	respect, worship, honor
Scapegoat	a person who is blamed for other's faults
Talisman	a charm or amulet with mystical or protective powers

NOW YOU TRY

Identify a synonym of the following words:

1. Belabor _____

2. Kindle _____

3. Debility _____

4. Innocuous _____

5. Abhor _____

6. Posthumous _____

7. Exacerbate _____

8. Talisman _____

9. Malady _____

10. Cerebral _____

11. Quarantine _____

12. Odious _____

13. Legend _____

14. Accolade _____

15. Mellow _____

16. Bristle _____

17. Diffident _____

18. Palisade _____

19. Arable _____

20. Recluse _____

21. Scapegoat _____

22. Expedite _____

23. Perjury _____

24. Revere _____

25. Enigma _____

ANSWERS

1. Explain
2. Ignite
3. Weakness
4. Harmless
5. Hate
6. Postmortem
7. Worsen
8. Charm
9. Illness
10. Intellectual
11. Isolate
12. Unpleasant
13. Myth, Key
14. Praise
15. Gentle
16. Stiffen
17. Reserved
18. Wall
19. Fertile
20. Loner
21. Excuse
22. Quicken
23. Lie
24. Respect
25. Mystery

VOCABULARY LIST #3

Abrogate	to repeal officially, cancel, nullify
Acrid	sharp or bitter smell, stinging or hurtful remark
Affable	likeable, friendly
Antiquated	old fashioned, ancient, out of date
Befuddle	confuse
Celerity	swiftness, speed
Certitude	without doubt
Confound	confuse
Deprecate	disapprove, denounce, judgmental
Droll	oddly or dryly funny
Epitomized	typified, embodied, exemplified
Exonerate	to free from blame, acquit
Garner	gather or collect
Heresy	blasphemy
Inadvertent	not on purpose, accidental, unintentional
Insatiable	not able to be satisfied or filled
Laceration	a cut
Liniment	soothing lotion
Magnanimous	forgiving, noble, generous
Meander	wander aimlessly
Myriad	many, a large number of
Pathos	persuasion which appeals to emotion
Peripheral	not central, unimportant, on the edge
Rescind	retract, repeal, invalidate
Rife	frequent, common, plentiful

NOW YOU TRY

Fill in the blanks in the following sentences using the word bank below:

Abrogate	Acrid	Affable	Antiquated	Befuddled
Celerity	Certitude	Confound	Deprecate	Droll
Epitomized	Exonerates	Garner	Heresy	Inadvertent
Insatiable	Laceration	Liniment	Magnanimous	Meander
Myriad	Pathos	Peripheral	Rescind	Rife

1. Because he felt bad after insulting his friend, he decided to _____ his prior statement.
2. In anticipation of the coming drought, all of the people in the city worked to _____ grain.
3. The teacher taught with _____ that the earth was not at the center of the universe.
4. Rather than researching directions, the family decided to _____ throughout the countryside on their vacation.
5. She needed to think deeply before deciding to _____ her order.
6. Due to his deep _____ the chef had to be rushed to the hospital for stitches.
7. After three hours the committee finally moved from _____ issues to those which were most important.
8. The mother told her daughter that it was not acceptable for her to _____ her little brother.
9. The beauty queen _____ the values of honesty and genuineness that the judges were looking for.
10. The electrician's _____ methods were slow and inefficient.
11. The woman was known and loved at the homeless shelter for her helpful and _____ disposition.
12. The man had many friends due to his _____ nature.
13. Horrified by her _____ mistake, the woman apologized repeatedly for getting in the wrong car.
14. After not eating all day, the man was _____ at dinner.
15. The child finished their assignment with _____ so that they could go outside and play.
16. The English teacher instructed her students to employ _____ in their essays.
17. The competitor was _____ by the instructions given by the referee.
18. The man was dreaded at parties for his _____ humor.
19. The earthquake caused a _____ of problems with the city's infrastructure.
20. Because of the rash that had developed on the patient's arm, the doctor proscribed a _____.
21. The dish's _____ smell made it inedible to the customer.

22. When the youth turned 18, the judge decided to _____ him and to clear his record.
23. After the house had been empty for 20 years, it was _____ with rodents.
24. Throughout history, many individuals who confronted the Catholic Church were condemned for _____.
25. In the chess match, the man was hoping to _____ his opponent.

ANSWERS

1. Rescind
2. Garner
3. Certitude
4. Meander
5. Abrogate
6. Laceration
7. Peripheral
8. Deprecate
9. Epitomized
10. Antiquated
11. Magnanimous
12. Affable
13. Inadvertent
14. Insatiable
15. Celerity
16. Pathos
17. Befuddled
18. Droll
19. Myriad
20. Liniment
21. Acrid
22. Exonerate
23. Rife
24. Heresy
25. Confound

VOCABULARY LIST #4

Advocate	argue in favor of, plead on behalf of
Amiable	kind, good-natured, friendly
Begrudge	resent, blame
Belie	contradict, misrepresent
Cacophony	unharmonious, loud noise
Candid	blunt, honest, frank
Credible	reliable, believable
Decorum	dignified, appropriate behavior
Didactic	preachy, instructive
Enshroud	cover
Expedient	necessary
Fickle	easily changed, unstable
Harangue	angry, attacking language
Illusory	deceptive, illusion, misleading
Indifferent	neutral
Irascible	quick to anger, hot-tempered
Laconic	quiet, brief
Marsupial	pouched mammal
Olfactory	relating to smell
Ornate	lavish, rich decoration
Paradox	apparently contradictory statement
Plumage	feathers of a bird
Potable	clean, drinkable
Raucous	harsh, rough, rowdy
Reprieve	temporary relief, respite

NOW YOU TRY

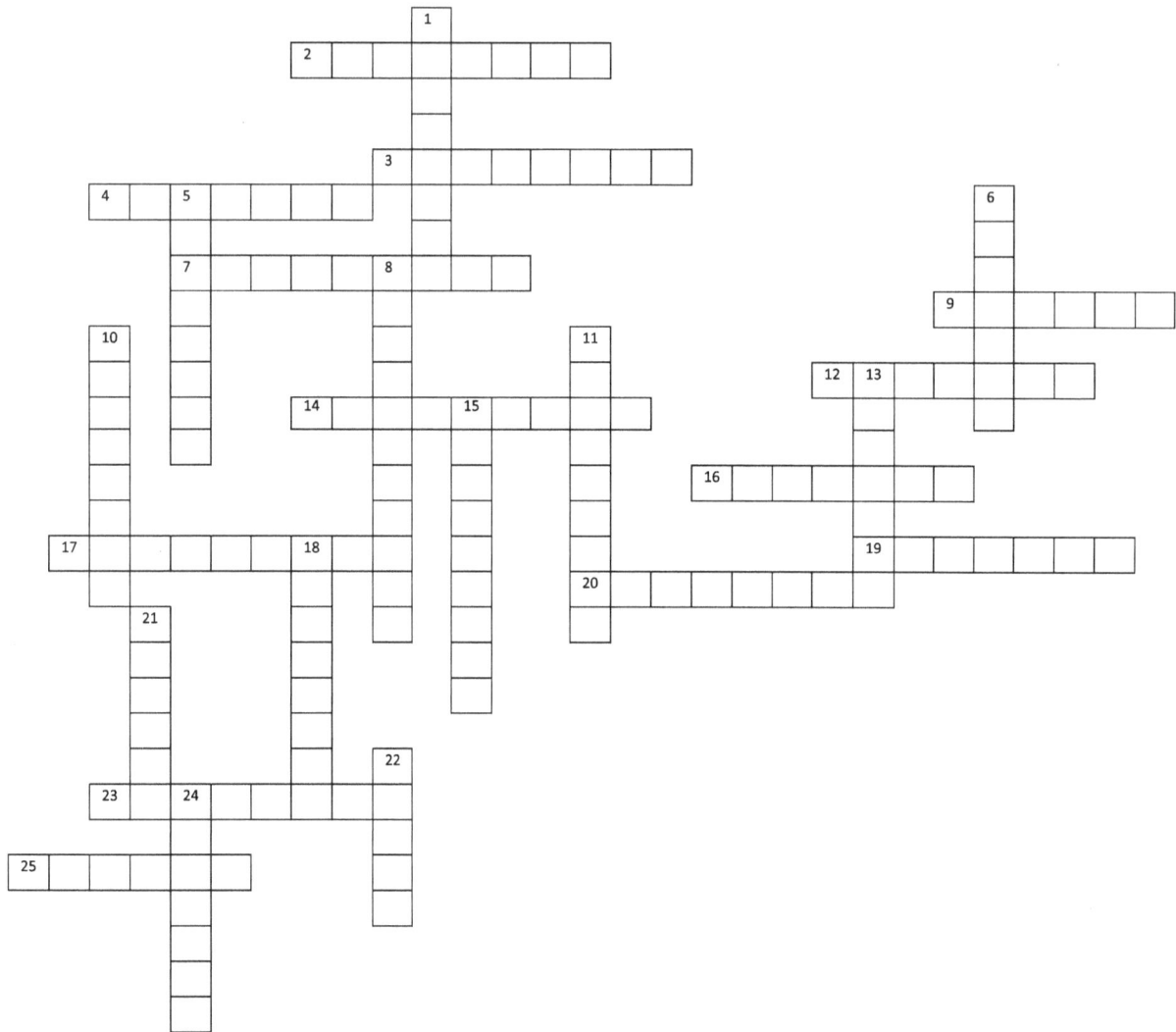

Across

2. preachy
3. cover
4. appropriate behavior
7. necessary
9. blunt, frank
12. harsh rowdy
14. relating to smell
16. fathers of a bird
17. quick to anger
19. quiet, brief
20. argue in favor of
23. respite
25. lavish, rich decoration

Down

1. angry, attacking language
5. believable
6. apparently contradictory statement
8. neutral
10. deceptive, misleading
11. pouched mammal
13. kind, friendly
15. unharmonious noise
18. blame, resent
21. easily changed, unstable
22. contradict, misrepresent
24. drinkable

ANSWERS

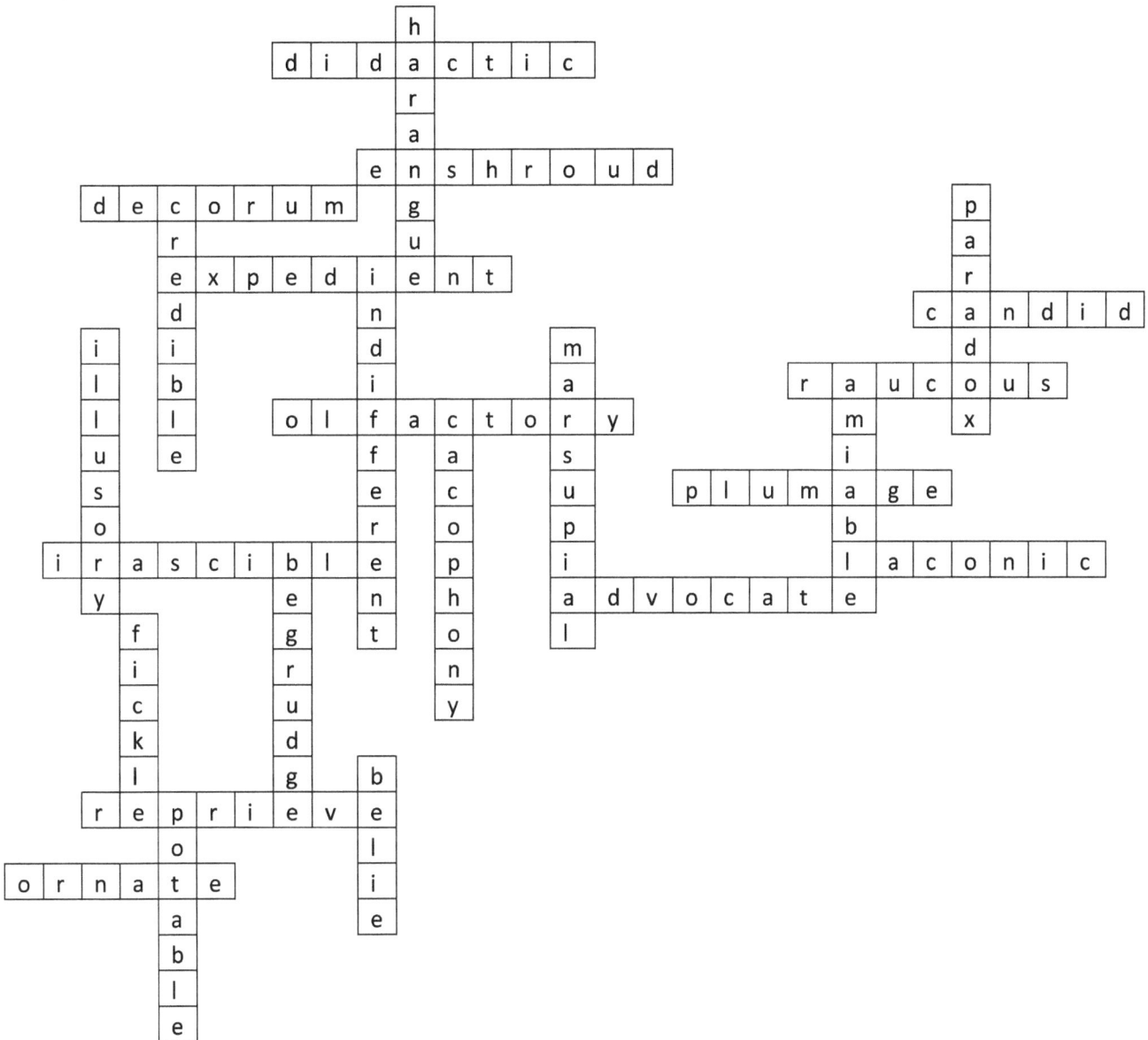

VOCABULARY LIST #5

Abrasive	coarse, harsh material; critical, aggressive
Acquiesce	to give in to
Apathetic	indifferent, uncaring
Blasphemy	impious, irreverent, forbidden speech
Capitulate	surrender
Charlatan	fake, liar, trickster, imposter
Condescend	looking down on
Credulous	gullible, trusting
Devoured	quickly and completely consumed
Discursiveness	rambling, chatty, long-winded
Equivocate	misleading, ambiguous, unclear expressions
Err	make a mistake
Finesse	graceful, skilled, poised
Hamper	hinder
Hyperbole	exaggeration
Ignominy	shame
Inertia	inactivity or momentum
Ire	anger
Lavish	grand, ornate, wasteful
Luscious	pleasant, luxurious, succulent, moist
Lynch	to kill illegally by hanging
Misogynist	hater of women
Obdurate	stubborn, not moved by conscience
Officious	domineering, meddlesome, forward
Palpable	able to be felt, tangible

NOW YOU TRY

Match the word with its definition:

1. Abrasive	a. impious, irreverent speech
2. Acquiesce	b. hinder
3. Apathetic	c. rambling, chatty, long-winded
4. Blasphemy	d. misleading, ambiguous, unclear expressions
5. Capitulate	e. critical, aggressive
6. Charlatan	f. hater of women
7. Condescend	g. exaggeration
8. Credulous	h. able to be felt, tangible
9. Devoured	i. fake, liar, imposter
10. Discursiveness	j. inactivity or momentum
11. Equivocate	k. pleasant, luxurious, moist
12. Err	l. to give in to
13. Finesse	m. gullible, trusting
14. Hamper	n. quickly and completely consumed
15. Hyperbole	o. stubborn, not moved by conscience
16. Ignominy	p. looking down on
17. Inertia	q. indifferent, uncaring
18. Ire	r. anger
19. Lavish	s. surrender
20. Luscious	t. grand, ornate, wasteful
21. Lynch	u. domineering, meddlesome, forward
22. Misogynist	v. make a mistake
23. Obdurate	w. shame
24. Officious	x. graceful, skilled, poised
25. Palpable	y. to kill illegally by hanging

ANSWERS

1. e
2. l
3. q
4. a
5. s
6. i
7. p
8. m
9. n
10. c
11. d
12. v
13. x
14. b
15. g
16. w
17. j
18. r
19. t
20. k
21. y
22. f
23. o
24. u
25. h

VOCABULARY LIST #6

Disdain	contempt, scorn
Feasible	possible, practical
Headstrong	stubborn
Inconsequential	unimportant
Irrevocable	unalterable, cannot be canceled
Lummox	clumsy person
Monotonous	tedious, boring, repetitive
Overwrought	elaborate or excessive emotion, excitement or agitation
Perfidy	an act of treachery
Plausible	believable, feasible, possible
Potent	strong, powerful; persuasive
Proponents	supporters, advocates
Quirk	oddity
Reprehensible	blameworthy, shameful
Sagacious	wise, all-knowing
Serendipity	fortunate coincidence, lucky accidental discovery
Stifle	suppress
Succinct	brief, clear, concise
Tenuous	fragile, easily broken
Torpid	dull, slow, sluggish
Unctuous	oily, greasy; smug piousness, flattery
Unprecedented	unexpected, unusual occurrence
Volatile	unstable, unpredictable
Wane	reduce in size
Waylay	ambush, accost unexpectedly

NOW YOU TRY

List an antonym (opposite) for each of the following words:

1. Disdain   _____
2. Feasible   _____
3. Headstrong   _____
4. Inconsequential   _____
5. Irrevocable   _____
6. Lummox   _____
7. Monotonous   _____
8. Overwrought   _____
9. Perfidy   _____
10. Plausible   _____
11. Potent   _____
12. Proponents   _____
13. Quirk   _____
14. Reprehensible   _____
15. Sagacious   _____
16. Serendipity   _____
17. Stifle   _____
18. Succinct   _____
19. Tenuous   _____
20. Torpid   _____
21. Unctuous   _____
22. Unprecedented   _____
23. Volatile   _____
24. Wane   _____
25. Waylay   _____

ANSWERS

1. Respect
2. Impractical
3. Laidback
4. Important
5. Alterable
6. Graceful
7. Exciting
8. Muted
9. Loyalty
10. Impossible
11. Subtle
12. Opponents
13. Stereotype
14. Commendable
15. Foolish
16. Misfortune
17. Exacerbate
18. Wordy
19. Durable
20. Swift
21. Sincere
22. Expected
23. Predictable
24. Wax
25. Allow forward

VOCABULARY LIST #7

Cynical	expected selfish motives in others
Deference	respect
Deter	hinder, waylay, prevent
Eccentric	odd, quirky
Envenom	fill with venom; make bitter
Extrinsic	outward; not essential
Histrionic	theatrical, over the top actions
Indolence	idle, laziness
Irrational	illogical, unreasonable
Longevity	long life
Loquacious	talkative, chatty
Mallet	wooden hammer
Nullify	cancel, legally void
Obsequious	submissive, attentive, brown-nosing
Ostentatious	flashy, showy
Patron	supporter, fan
Pliable	flexible, movable
Pragmatic	practical
Prodigal	wasteful, lavish
Puerile	immature, childish
Recapitulate	brief summary
Retention	preservation; recollection
Sage	wise
Solace	comfort (for grieving person)
Substantiate	establish, affirm, give evidence

NOW YOU TRY

Fill in the blanks in the sentences using the words from the following word bank:

Cynical	Deference	Deter	Eccentric	Envenom
Extrinsic	Histrionic	Indolence	Irrational	Longevity
Loquacious	Mallet	Nullify	Obsequious	Ostentatious
Patron	Pliable	Pragmatic	Prodigal	Puerile
Recapitulate	Retention	Sage	Solace	Substantiate

1. He makes a good entertainer because of his _____ nature and upbeat personality.
2. The restaurant manager fired the server because of his _____, speed, and often forgot entire tables.
3. Although normally he was proud of his nice car, he worried that it would be too _____ in the run-down neighborhood that he was driving through.
4. In Korean culture it is essential to show _____ to one's elders.
5. Many people went to the priest when they had problems to seek his _____ advice.
6. Bamboo is often used in constructing the backs of chairs because it is such a _____ material.
7. Because their son was so _____, the parents decided to cut him out of their will.
8. The competitor decided that he was not going to allow his past mistakes to _____ him from trying his hardest to win the competition.
9. The teacher explained to her students that it would be _____ to expect to get good grades if they did not complete all of their assignments.
10. After giving the student feedback about their presentation, the teacher asked them to _____ the advice that she had offered to be sure they were listening.
11. When the woman learned that the company was not legally accredited she immediately decided to _____ her contract with them.
12. Her _____ nature made her untrusting and critical of others.
13. At his hundredth birthday the man attributed his _____ to good diet and exercise in his youth.
14. The trial was lost because the plaintiff could not _____ his claims.
15. She was praised for her _____ of information when she was able to recite the figures perfectly.
16. Although Sally was frustrated by Tom's bitter attitude, not wanting to _____ him further she held her tongue.
17. The woman was in need of _____ after the death of her husband.
18. The other students called John a teacher's pet because of his _____ air.
19. Young children are often more motivated by _____ rewards and punishments than by conscience.

20. Victorian design can often become _____ because it incorporates so many different factors.
21. It was very _____ of the lawyer to get so angry when he lost the case.
22. The judged banged his _____ and ordered to court to silence after the client's outburst.
23. The art _____ spent two million dollars on the famous piece of art.
24. The woman displayed her frustration with a _____ display of anger.
25. People often asked Lisa for her advice because she was _____ and logical.

ANSWERS

1. Loquacious
2. Indolence
3. Ostentatious
4. Deference
5. Sage
6. Pliable
7. Prodigal
8. Deter
9. Irrational
10. Recapitulate
11. Nullify
12. Cynical
13. Longevity
14. Substantiate
15. Retention
16. Envenom
17. Solace
18. Obsequious
19. Extrinsic
20. Eccentric
21. Puerile
22. Mallet
23. Patron
24. Histrionic
25. Pragmatic

VOCABULARY LIST #8

Altruism	kindness, selflessness, caring
Beguile	trick, deceive, mislead
Bulwark	defense, barricade, wall
Cajole	coax, convince
Depravity	corrupt, evil, bad
Enfranchise	to give voting rights
Fecund	fertile, fruitful
Goad	encourage, urge; poke, prod
Hypocritical	when actions are not in line with vocalizations
Incessant	continuous
Jaded	dulled, worn out, tired
Knotty	full of knots; complex, intricate, difficult
Lithe	limber, flexible, pliant
Manipulatable	manageable, easily controlled
Noxious	poisonous, harmful
Obstreperous	difficult to control; noisy
Palatable	acceptable; edible
Quandary	dilemma
Raze	to destroy, tear down
Savant	genius
Tangible	real, physical, can be touched
Utopia	perfect society
Vindicate	avenge, remove blame
Wary	cautious, suspicious
Weighty	important, serious

NOW YOU TRY

List an antonym (opposite) for each of the words below:

1. Altruism   _____
2. Beguile   _____
3. Bulwark   _____
4. Cajole   _____
5. Depravity   _____
6. Enfranchise   _____
7. Fecund   _____
8. Goad   _____
9. Hypocritical   _____
10. Incessant   _____
11. Jaded   _____
12. Knotty   _____
13. Lithe   _____
14. Manipulatable   _____
15. Noxious   _____
16. Obstreperous   _____
17. Palatable   _____
18. Quandary   _____
19. Raze   _____
20. Savant   _____
21. Tangible   _____
22. Utopia   _____
23. Vindicate   _____
24. Wary   _____
25. Weighty   _____

ANSWERS

1. Selfishness
2. Encourage
3. Opening
4. Force
5. Transparent
6. Disenfranchise
7. Sterile
8. Discourage
9. Sincere
10. Sporadic
11. Sharp
12. Simple
13. Stiff
14. Uncontrollable
15. Healthy
16. Manageable
17. Inedible
18. Solution
19. Build
20. Fool
21. Intangible
22. Anarchy
23. Pardon
24. Heedless
25. Unimportant

VOCABULARY LIST #9

Adversity	trial, hardship
Balk	hesitate
Cartographer	person who makes maps
Cringe	shrink away, recoil
Demur	object, refuse
Derogatory	offensive, hurtful, to put down
Dike	dam
Elucidate	clarify, explain
Epistle	letter
Flaunt	show off
Futile	hopeless
Germane	relevant, pertinent
Inclination	disposition, tendency
Infallible	flawless, perfect
Laud	praise
Parched	dried up, thirsty
Perpetuated	continued
Pertinent	relevant
Portend	foreshadow
Pristine	clear, clean, untouched
Respite	break
Scale	to climb; a weighing tool
Stupefying	shocking, stunning
Thwart	prevent
Truant	absent without permission

NOW YOU TRY

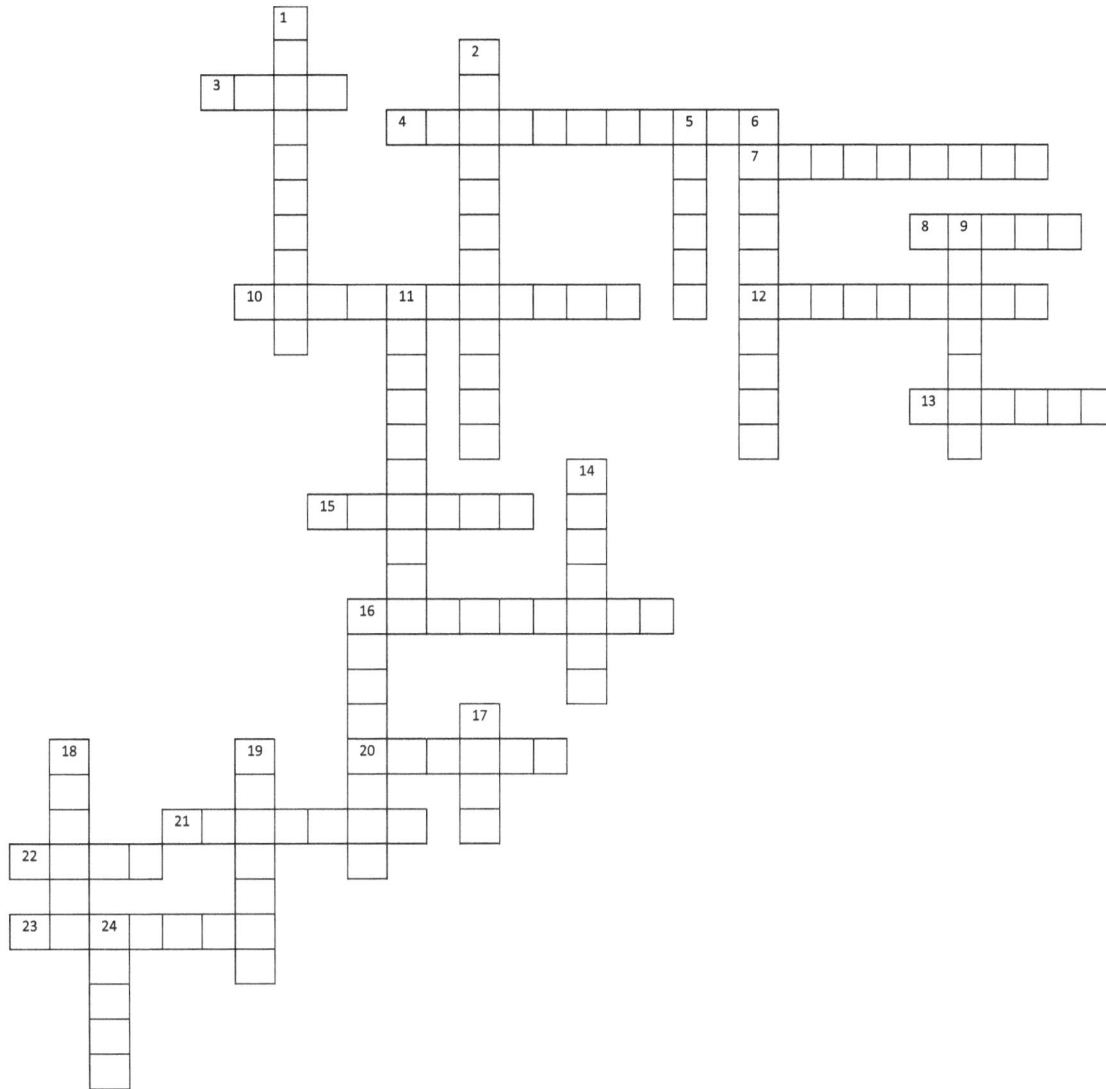

Across

3. praise
4. continued
7. clarify, explain
8. object, refuse
10. disposition, tendency
12. trial, hardship
13. show off
15. shrink away, recoil
16. relevant
20. prevent
21. relevant, pertinent
22. dam
23. break

Down

1. shocking, stunning
2. person who makes maps
5. absent without permission
6. offensive, hurt, put down
9. letter
11. flawless, perfect
14. foreshadow
16. clear, clean, untouched
17. hesitate
18. hopeless
19. dried up, thirsty
24. climb; weighing tool

ANSWERS

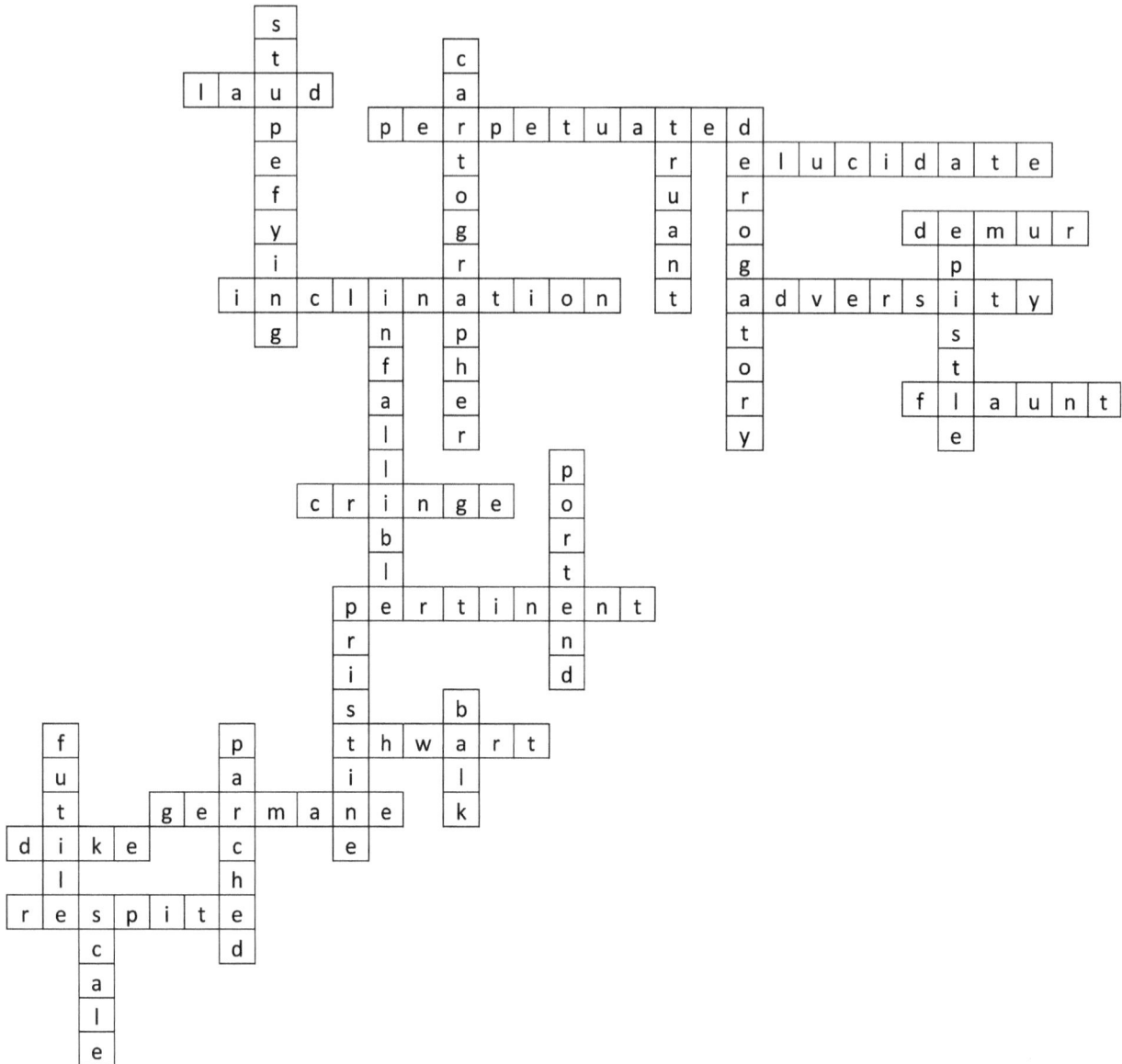

VOCABULARY LIST #10

Analogous	comparable, similar, corresponding
Antediluvian	old-fashioned, primitive
Bigot	biased, prejudiced person
Burgeon	flourish, grow
Colloquial	informal, regional language
Counterfeit	falsified, fake documents
Deliberate	on purpose; to consider deeply
Edifice	building
Ephemeral	short-lived, temporary
Exemplary	commendable, outstanding, good example
Gratuitous	without reason or justification; bestowed voluntarily
Hinder	obstruct, prevent
Incarceration	putting in prison
Irreproachable	flawless
Lampoon	satirical, ridiculing literature
Ludicrous	ridiculous, absurd
Misnomer	inappropriate or erring name
Mutinous	rebellious
Onus	difficult task
Oust	expel, evict, remove from position
Parody	satirical imitation, spoof
Platitudes	dull, trite remarks
Predecessor	one who came before
Profound	significant, meaningful
Ruse	trick, misleading action

NOW YOU TRY

Match the word with its definition.

1. Analogous	a. comparable, similar, corresponding
2. Antediluvian	b. flourish, grow
3. Bigot	c. trick, misleading action
4. Burgeon	d. expel, evict, remove from position
5. Colloquial	e. putting in prison
6. Counterfeit	f. old-fashioned, primitive
7. Deliberate	g. building
8. Edifice	h. flawless
9. Ephemeral	i. difficult task
10. Exemplary	j. significant, meaningful
11. Gratuitous	k. informal, regional language
12. Hinder	l. rebellious
13. Incarceration	m. one who came before
14. Irreproachable	n. on purpose; to consider deeply
15. Lampoon	o. biased, prejudiced person
16. Ludicrous	p. without reason or justification; bestowed voluntarily
17. Misnomer	q. satirical, ridiculing literature
18. Mutinous	r. short-lived, temporary
19. Onus	s. satirical imitation, spoof
20. Oust	t. ridiculous, absurd
21. Parody	u. falsified, fake documents
22. Platitudes	v. inappropriate or erring name
23. Predecessor	w. commendable, outstanding, good example
24. Profound	x. dull, trite remarks
25. Ruse	y. obstruct, prevent

ANSWERS

1. a
2. f
3. o
4. b
5. k
6. u
7. n
8. g
9. r
10. w
11. p
12. y
13. e
14. h
15. q
16. t
17. v
18. l
19. i
20. d
21. s
22. x
23. m
24. j
25. c

VOCABULARY LIST #11

Complacent	pleased, self-assured, smug
Diatribes	bitter attack or criticism
Esoteric	obscure, confidential, revealed to select few
Hone	sharpen, increase
Lethargic	tired, worn-out
Modicum	small amount
Negligence	carelessness
Oblique	slanting, sloping, not straight
Opulent	rich, wealthy, ornate and lavish
Picayune	small, of little value
Precarious	unstable, on edge, risky
Presumptuous	arrogant in assumptions, bold
Querulous	always complaining
Resplendent	shining, gleaming, glowing
Sallow	sickly yellowish color
Skirmish	minor battle
Subterfuge	trickery, deception, undermining
Tenacious	stubborn, persistent, tough
Tranquil	calm, peaceful, serene
Traverse	to move across
Trite	overused, boring
Underscore	emphasize importance of
Vagrant	homeless wanderer
Vehemence	fervor, vigorous, forceful
Voracious	starving, ravenous

NOW YOU TRY

List a synonym (a word with close or the same meaning) for each of the following words:

1. Complacent

   _____

2. Diatribes

   _____

3. Esoteric

   _____

4. Hone

   _____

5. Lethargic

   _____

6. Degree

   _____

7. Negligence

   _____

8. Oblique

   _____

9. Opulent

   _____

10. Picayune

    _____

11. Precarious

    _____

12. Presumptuous

    _____

13. Querulous

    _____

14. Resplendent

    _____

15. Sallow

    _____

16. Skirmish

    _____

17. Subterfuge

    _____

18. Tenacious

    _____

19. Tranquil

    _____

20. Traverse

    _____

21. Trite

    _____

22. Underscore

    _____

23. Vagrant

    _____

24. Vehemence

    _____

25. Voracious

    _____

ANSWERS

1. Satisfied
2. Attacks
3. Obscure
4. Sharpen
5. Tired
6. Degree
7. Neglect
8. Tilted
9. Lavish
10. Small
11. Perilous
12. Arrogant
13. Argumentative
14. Brilliant
15. Wan
16. Scuffle
17. Maneuver
18. Stubborn
19. Serene
20. Navigate
21. Commonplace
22. Emphasize
23. Itinerant
24. Intensity
25. Starving

VOCABULARY LIST #12

Aesthetic	relating to art, beauty, and sensation
Animosity	strong dislike, antagonism, ill will
Brevity	brief
Caustic	burning, corrosive; biting, hurtful
Circumvent	avoid
Degradation	humiliation; poverty
Diligent	hard-working, persistent, determined
Egregious	glaringly, obviously bad
Fanaticism	passion, devotion
Gambol	frolic, skipping about
Impromptu	spontaneous, spur-of-the-moment
Languish	lose vitality, become weak, fade
Magnate	influential person, powerful businessman
Matriarchy	society governed by women
Nebulous	vague, indistinct, fuzzy
Omniscient	all-knowing
Perspicacity	mental acuity, insight
Ponderous	heavy, awkward; dull
Precipitous	abrupt, rushed; sheer, steep
Resolution	determination; formal decision made by a governing group
Sanction	approval or permission from authority
Somnambulist	sleepwalker
Tedium	boredom
Trivial	unimportant, insignificant
Usurp	to take without right

NOW YOU TRY

Fill in the blanks in each of the following sentences using one of the words in the word bank:

Aesthetic	Animosity	Brevity	Caustic	Circumvent
Degradation	Diligent	Egregious	Fanaticism	Gambol
Impromptu	Languish	Magnate	Matriarchy	Nebulous
Omniscient	Perspicacity	Ponderous	Precipitous	Resolution
Sanction	Somnambulist	Tedium	Trivial	Usurp

1. The lawyer hoped to _____ filling out the extra paperwork by speaking directly with the judge.
2. On his birthday, the manager was asked to give an _____ speech when the office surprised him with a cake.
3. Parliament passed the new _____ by an overwhelming majority.
4. Her _____ towards her boss made it impossible for her to continue working at the firm.
5. The band's admirers displayed such _____ that it became necessary for them to call the police to hold them back.
6. Everyone quieted in respect and awe as the _____ entered the room.
7. The man struggled to carry his _____ load up the stairs and into his apartment.
8. The design had a pleasing _____ quality that made its creator famous.
9. It became necessary for the company to take its office to lunch to break up the _____ of the work week.
10. Michelangelo painted the ceilings of the Sistine Chapel by official _____ of the Pope.
11. The day after a bitter fight, each of the friends apologized for their _____ remarks the day before.
12. After murdering his neighbor, the man was sentenced to _____ in jail for 20 years.
13. Due to time constraints, the speaker was forced to give their speech in a _____ manner.
14. Her _____ allowed her to see that what the child really needed was attention.
15. _____ was the downfall of the executive: she was fired because she could not explain herself.
16. After declaring bankruptcy and losing his business, the man fell into a state of _____.
17. It was too dangerous for her to sleep on a bunk bed because she was a _____.
18. The man apologized profusely for his _____ error after turning into oncoming traffic.

19. Anyone who saw the two interact knew that the couple operated as a _____.
20. The psychic claimed to be _____; however, few people were impressed with her skills.
21. The medical student was upset to find that on the new software, the brain appeared as a gray _____ cloud, rather than being distinct enough to identify.
22. The executive became frustrated when his committee focused the meeting on _____ issues, rather than focusing on how to increase efficiency in the next quarter.
23. Thanks to the student's _____ efforts, the group was able to receive an A on their project.
24. The rival king was thwarted in his attempt to _____ control of the kingdom through war.
25. Although there were games and toys to play with, the children were content to _____ on the grass.

ANSWERS

1. Circumvent
2. Impromptu
3. Resolution
4. Animosity
5. Fanaticism
6. Magnate
7. Ponderous
8. Aesthetic
9. Tedium
10. Sanction
11. Caustic
12. Languish
13. Precipitous
14. Perspicacity
15. Brevity
16. Degradation
17. Somnambulist
18. Egregious
19. Matriarchy
20. Omniscient
21. Nebulous
22. Trivial
23. Diligent
24. Usurp
25. Gambol

VOCABULARY LIST #13

Absolution	forgive, free from blame, pardon
Attenuate	reduce; weaken
Boorish	crude, insensitive, ill-mannered
Chicanery	deception, trickery
Concatenation	linking into chains
Disapprobation	disapproval, condemnation
Eulogy	praise of a deceased person
Furrow	wrinkle, groove
Germinal	undeveloped, in the early stages of growth
Idiosyncrasy	habits, quirks, mannerisms, personal peculiarity
Inebriation	drunkenness; intoxication
Moribund	stagnant; near death
Oblivious	completely unaware
Opaque	solid, not transparent
Parity	equality, similarity
Peremptory	in a commanding manner, not allowing debate
Poseur	someone who puts on an act, acts different to impress others
Ramble	wandering, winding path, aimless
Reticent	reserved, restrained
Salubrious	promoting health, health-giving
Sensuous	appealing to the senses
Strident	harsh, grating, shrill
Totter	sway, shake, walk unsteadily
Tumult	uproar, riot, disorder
Voluble	talkative; continuous flow of words

NOW YOU TRY

List an antonym (opposite) for each of the following words:

1. Absolution   _____

2. Attenuate   _____

3. Boorish   _____

4. Chicanery   _____

5. Concatenation   _____

6. Disapprobation   _____

7. Eulogy   _____

8. Furrow   _____

9. Germinal   _____

10. Idiosyncrasy   _____

11. Inebriation   _____

12. Moribund   _____

13. Oblivious   _____

14. Opaque   _____

15. Parity   _____

16. Peremptory   _____

17. Poseur   _____

18. Ramble   _____

19. Reticent   _____

20. Salubrious   _____

21. Sensuous   _____

22. Strident   _____

23. Totter   _____

24. Tumult   _____

25. Voluble   _____

ANSWERS

1. Condemnation
2. Strengthen
3. Courteous
4. Forthrightness
5. Raze
6. Support
7. Criticism
8. Smooth
9. Grown
10. Stereotype
11. Sober
12. Vivacious
13. Attuned
14. Transparent
15. Variation
16. Submissive
17. Sincere
18. With purpose
19. Wild
20. Noxious
21. Dull
22. Soft
23. Taut
24. Peace
25. Laconic

VOCABULARY LIST #14

Abstain	go without, refrain, deny oneself
Appease	sooth, satisfy, make calm
Blighted	damaged, impaired, destroyed
Cantankerous	ill-tempered, ornery, quarrelsome
Compliant	easygoing, submissive
Deplete	use up
Discrepancy	irregularity, when something doesn't match up
Engender	cause
Execrable	abhorrent, bad, abominable
Fastidious	critical, demanding; requiring care
Garble	confuse, jumble, distort
Hedonist	a person who pursues self-gratification
Intermittent	sporadic, random, irregular
Largess	generosity, bestowal of gifts
Momentous	extremely important
Obscure	vague, unclear; hidden
Obviate	anticipate, prevent; make unnecessary
Paragon	perfect example, model, pattern of
Parsimonious	stingy, thrifty
Pervasive	spreading everywhere
Precinct	a city district
Proscribe	forbid, denounce, condemn
Rotund	round, plump
Scrutinize	carefully examine
Stolid	unemotional, dull, indifferent

NOW YOU TRY

Complete the analogies using one of the words in the following word bank:

Abstain	Appease	Blighted	Cantankerous	Compliant
Deplete	Discrepancy	Engender	Execrable	Fastidious
Garble	Hedonist	Intermittent	Largess	Momentous
Obscure	Obviate	Paragon	Parsimonious	Pervasive
Precinct	Proscribed	Rotund	Scrutinize	Stolid

Example: Finger: Hand:: Petal: Flower. These compare the relationship from part to whole.

1. Small: Belittle:: Calm: _____
2. Up: Down:: Lovely: _____
3. Isolated: _____:: Tumult: Peace
4. Moderation: Thin:: Indulgence: _____
5. Negligence: Neglect:: Important: _____
6. _____: Jumble:: Arrange: Organize
7. Easygoing: _____:: Resistant: Defiant
8. Prudent: Wasteful:: _____: Extravagant
9. Continuous: Incessant:: Sporadic: _____
10. Forbid: Outlaw:: _____: Cause
11. Cursory: Hurried Examination:: Thorough: _____
12. Pain: Masochist:: Self-gratification: _____
13. Battle: Skirmish:: Irregularity: _____
14. Noxious: Harmful:: _____: Generous
15. Starving: Ravenous:: Refrain: _____
16. Neighborhood: _____: Country: Nation
17. Perceive: Perspicacity:: Anticipate: _____
18. Sustain: Maintain:: _____: Use up
19. Exercise: Recommended:: Drugs: _____
20. Interested: Attentive:: Indifferent: _____
21. Uncover: Illuminate:: Hide: _____
22. East: West:: Perfect Condition:: _____
23. Quarrelsome: _____:: Accord: Agreement
24. _____: Critical:: Mutinous: Rebellious
25. Example: _____:: Dilemma: Quandary

ANSWERS

1. Appease
2. Execrable
3. Pervasive
4. Rotund
5. Momentous
6. Garble
7. Compliant
8. Parsimonious
9. Intermittent
10. Engender
11. Scrutinize
12. Hedonist
13. Discrepancy
14. Largess
15. Abstain
16. Precinct
17. Obviate
18. Deplete
19. Proscribed
20. Stolid
21. Obscure
22. Blighted
23. Cantankerous
24. Fastidious
25. Paragon

VOCABULARY LIST #15

Arcane	understood by few
Austere	very dull, plain, unadorned
Burnish	polish, make smooth
Catharsis	emotional relief or peace
Connoisseur	expert, refined person
Cryptic	confusing, must be deciphered
Discord	disagreement
Exhaustive	thorough, complete
Haughtiness	pride
Incoherent	not understandable, confusing, unclear
Inveterate	habitual
Lackluster	not exciting, dull, monotonous
Marred	damaged, imperfect
Morose	ill-humored, moody, sad
Overt	obvious
Percipient	insightful, discerning
Petulant	showing irritation, sulky
Poignant	keen, strong
Preamble	introduction
Preeminent	superior, outstanding
Protagonist	main character
Sanguine	happy, cheerful, calm
Staunch	devout, loyal
Supercilious	arrogant, haughty
Unequivocal	clear, obvious

NOW YOU TRY

Using the words in the following word bank, fill in the blanks in the sentences:

Arcane	Austere	Burnished	Catharsis	Connoisseur
Cryptic	Discord	Exhaustive	Haughtiness	Incoherent
Inveterate	Lackluster	Marred	Morose	Overt
Percipient	Petulant	Poignant	Preamble	Preeminent
Protagonist	Sanguine	Staunch	Supercilious	Unequivocal

1. The museum was proud to hire the new curator because he was such a well-known _____ of art.
2. Although the school always encouraged confidence in their graduates, the girl's _____ and arrogance astounded the school board.
3. The perfume line was known for its subtle scents, so when their new perfume was rather _____, everyone was surprised by it.
4. Sally was upset by reviews criticizing her performance as _____ and dull.
5. After growing up in an Amish community, the family had developed a taste for _____ decoration.
6. Her _____ hatred of her neighbor made it impossible for them to continue living there.
7. The document's _____ identified the main points that it would be addressing.
8. The collector _____ his rocks twice a day to maintain their polished look.
9. The new office manager was efficient and organized. As a result, the office ran smoothly and the employees were _____.
10. The document was rewritten to ensure that its content was _____: the employee's behavior was unacceptable.
11. The politician's reputation was irrevocably _____ when it was discovered he'd had an affair.
12. The committee fell into _____ when they learned that salaries needed to be reduced.
13. After writing a long letter to her father, Jane finally reached a _____ about her troubled childhood.
14. Whenever the family recalled their mother's funeral, everyone became _____.
15. The child's _____ tone upset her parents, and they sent her to her room.
16. The new manager was a _____ advocate of reordering the schedules to achieve increased efficiency.
17. Although he left them a message when he left the house, it was so _____ that no one knew where he went.
18. Her detailed list of chores for the weekend was _____.

19. The man's wife left him because he was an _____ gambler, and lost their life savings after a weekend in Las Vegas.
20. Her favorite character in the novel was the _____, a poor boy left to fend for himself in the city.
21. Despite her excessive donations to the charity, she is not very well liked because of her _____ attitude.
22. The _____ judge was able to determine which of the parties was truly guilty.
23. After three hours, the committee finally moved to the _____ issue: how to increase profit.
24. The chess master's methods were _____ and, as a result, he rarely lost.
25. The toddler's speech was _____ to everyone but his mother.

ANSWERS

1. Connoisseur
2. Haughtiness
3. Poignant
4. Lackluster
5. Austere
6. Overt
7. Preamble
8. Burnished
9. Sanguine
10. Unequivocal
11. Marred
12. Discord
13. Catharsis
14. Morose
15. Petulant
16. Staunch
17. Cryptic
18. Exhaustive
19. Inveterate
20. Protagonist
21. Supercilious
22. Percipient
23. Preeminent
24. Arcane
25. Incoherent

VOCABULARY LIST #16

Belittle	demean, insult
Carping	critical, petty
Circuitous	circular, winding, indirect
Congeal	solidify
Defunct	obsolete, no longer in use or existence
Desecrate	to treat with sacrilege, pollute a holy place
Dilatory	delayed, procrastinate, slow
Dupe	to fool or trick
Euphemism	a more polite and correct way to say something
Garish	tasteless, showy, gaudy
Immoderate	excessive, not restrained
Indulgent	permissive, pampering
Interminable	incessant, never-ending
Livid	extremely angry
Meager	little, inadequate
Nuance	a subtle element
Ominous	foreboding, threatening
Peruse	thorough, careful reading
Prescient	perceptive, having foresight
Progenitor	ancestor
Renown	widespread fame, good reputation
Scuttle	scurry; quick, hurried steps
Tirade	prolonged angry speech
Thwart	prevent
Truant	absent without permission

NOW YOU TRY

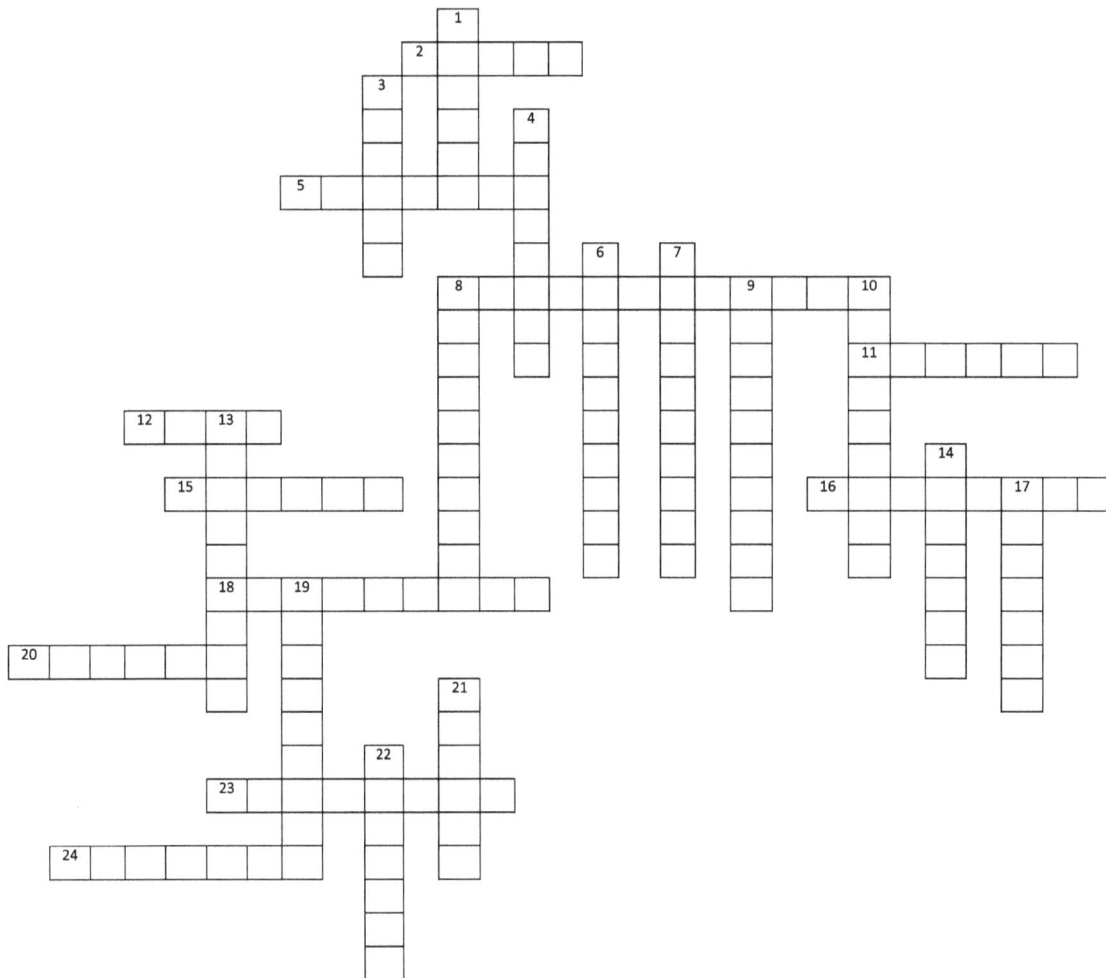

Across

2. extremely angry
5. solidify
8. incessant, never-ending
11. thorough, careful reading
12. to fool or trick
15. little, inadequate amount
16. delayed, slow
18. permissive, pampering
20. widespread fame, good reputation
23. pain reliever
24. scurry; quick, hurried steps

Down

1. prolonged angry speech
3. a subtle element
4. demean, insult
6. ancestor
7. circular, winding, indirect
8. excessive, not restrained
9. improve
10. a more polite way of saying something
13. perceptive, having foresight
14. critical petty
17. foreboding, threatening
19. to treat with sacrilege, disrespect something holy
21. tasteless, showy, gaudy
22. obsolete, no longer in use or existence

ANSWERS

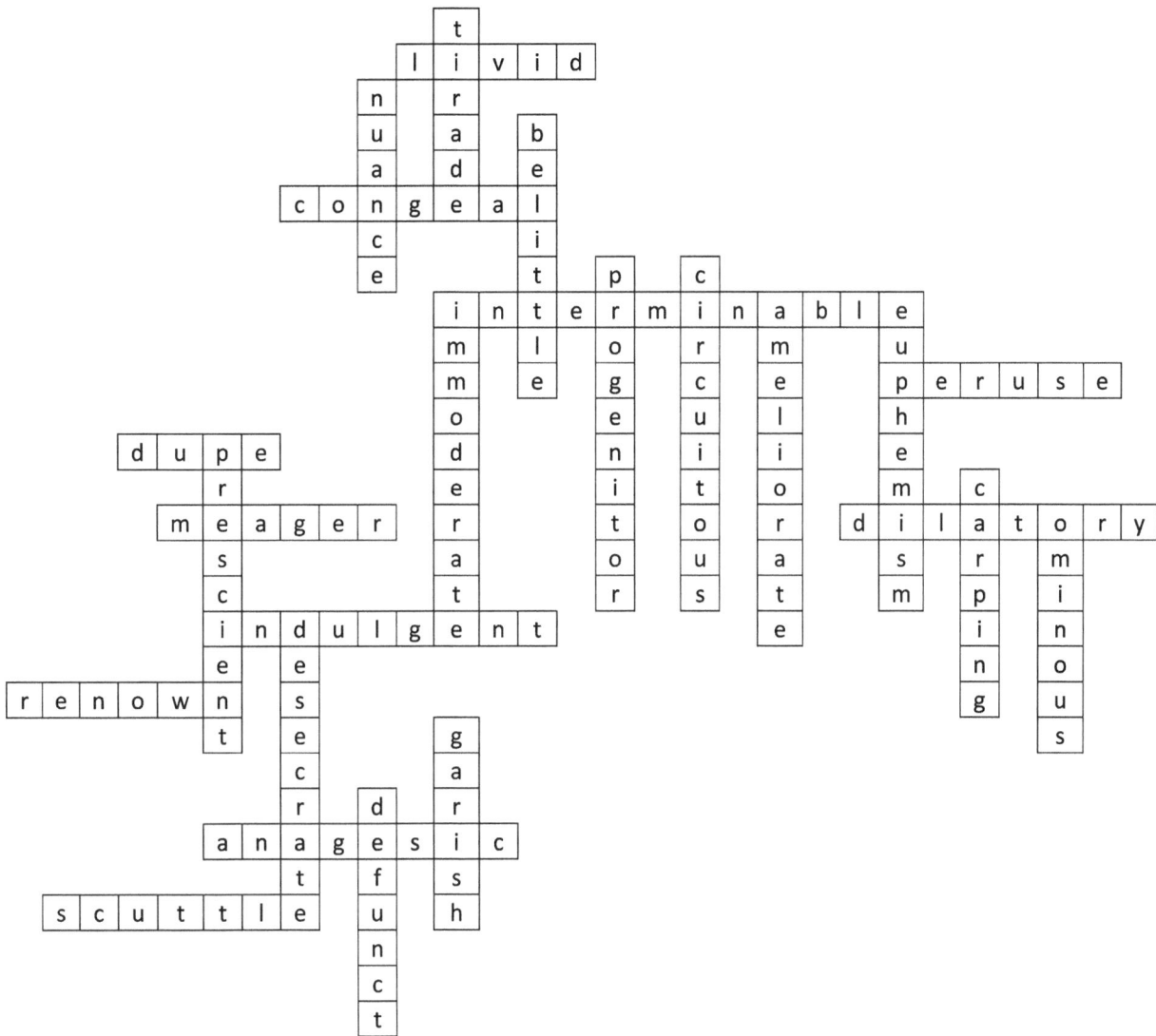

VOCABULARY LIST #17

Anecdote	a short narrative
Apathy	lacking emotion, uncaring, disinterested
Atheist	one who does not believe in God
Bane	something which brings ruin or distress
Broach	to approach or initiate; begin discussing
Censure	reprimand; blame
Concise	clear, direct, brief
Consensus	agreement
Despondent	discouraged, gloomy, hopeless
Destitution	poverty
Efface	erase, withdraw, remove
Eloquent	persuasive, forceful, fluent speech
Erratic	unusual, irregular, eccentric
Extraneous	irrelevant, extra
Gaunt	thin, emaciated
Irksome	annoying, frustrating, tiresome
Jargon	language specific to a certain skill
Mitigate	belittle
Negate	nullify, cancel
Obtuse	unobservant, dumb, dull
Ossify	harden; turn to bone
Paramount	very important, preeminent
Perpetual	endless, continual
Plethora	many, abundance, excess
Pretentious	acting above one's station; pompous, self-important, ostentatious

NOW YOU TRY

Match the word with its definition.

1. Anecdote	a. one who does not believe in God
2. Apathy	b. a short narrative
3. Atheist	c. irrelevant, extra
4. Bane	d. unobservant, dumb, dull
5. Broach	e. lacking emotion, uncaring, disinterested
6. Censure	f. endless, continual
7. Concise	g. discouraged, gloomy, hopeless
8. Consensus	h. reprimand; blame
9. Despondent	i. harden; turn to bone
10. Destitution	j. many, abundance, excess
11. Efface	k. to approach or initiate; begin discussing
12. Eloquent	l. thin, emaciated
13. Erratic	m. unusual, irregular, eccentric
14. Extraneous	n. language specific to a certain skill
15. Gaunt	o. agreement
16. Irksome	p. nullify, cancel
17. Jargon	q. something which brings ruin or distress
18. Mitigate	r. poverty
19. Negate	s. acting above one's station; pompous
20. Obtuse	t. annoying, frustrating, tiresome
21. Ossify	u. persuasive, forceful, fluent speech
22. Paramount	v. clear, direct, brief
23. Perpetual	w. very important, preeminent
24. Plethora	x. belittle
25. Pretentious	y. erase, withdraw, remove

ANSWERS

1. b
2. e
3. a
4. q
5. k
6. h
7. v
8. o
9. g
10. r
11. y
12. u
13. m
14. c
15. l
16. t
17. n
18. x
19. p
20. d
21. i
22. w
23. f
24. j
25. s

VOCABULARY LIST #18

Ambiguous	confusing, having multiple meanings
Anarchy	lack of government
Anomaly	oddity, unusual occurrence
Beneficiary	the person who benefits from an action or event
Bereavement	extreme grief over loss of loved one
Cloying	become distasteful by excess
Conflagration	fire
Deplore	censure; regret, lament
Dubious	doubtful
Euphony	harmonious, pleasant noise
Extol	to praise highly
Ignominious	degrading, shameful, humiliating
Incongruous	out of place
Intrepid	courageous, bold, brave
Invidious	intended to offend or create resentment
Lamentation	sorrow
Lucid	clear, easily understood, logical
Myopic	short-sighted, narrow-minded
Obliterate	destroy completely
Onerous	burdensome; irksome
Postulate	hypothesize
Prodigious	marvelous, large, abundant
Prolific	producing abundantly
Rancor	anger, resentment, hatred
Solicit	ask for, request, seek out

www.PassYourSAT.com

NOW YOU TRY

List a synonym (a word with close or the same meaning) for each of the following words:

1. Ambiguous   _____

2. Anarchy   _____

3. Anomaly   _____

4. Beneficiary   _____

5. Bereavement   _____

6. Cloying   _____

7. Conflagration   _____

8. Deplore   _____

9. Dubious   _____

10. Euphony   _____

11. Extol   _____

12. Ignominious   _____

13. Incongruous   _____

14. Intrepid   _____

15. Invidious   _____

16. Lamentation   _____

17. Lucid   _____

18. Myopic   _____

19. Obliterate   _____

20. Onerous   _____

21. Postulate   _____

22. Prodigious   _____

23. Prolific   _____

24. Rancor   _____

25. Solicit   _____

ANSWERS

1. Uncertain
2. Chaos
3. Abnormality
4. Benefactor
5. Grief
6. Saccharine
7. Fire
8. Detest
9. Doubtful
10. Harmonious
11. Praise
12. Infamous
13. Inconsistent
14. Valiant
15. Discriminatory
16. Sorrow
17. Articulate
18. Prejudiced
19. Destroy
20. Arduous
21. Theorize
22. Impressive
23. Inexhaustive
24. Malice
25. Petition

VOCABULARY LIST #19

Adroit	expert, skillful
Aloof	cold, distant, disinterested
Arbitrary	random
Augment	increase, enlarge
Blatant	obvious
Drivel	nonsense
Enhance	improve
Ensconce	secured, settled, settled in place
Gratis	free, pro bono
Hoary	grayish-white; white-haired; old
Inconspicuous	subtle, not noticeable
Infamous	hated, notorious, bad reputation
Malinger	to pretend illness to avoid work
Munificent	giving, generous
Pallid	pale
Placid	calm
Posterity	descendants
Profanity	swearing, cussing, irreverent language
Recant	to take back, denounce, retract
Skeptical	questioning, doubting
Subversive	rebellious, treacherous
Terse	abrupt, brusque, concise
Trepidation	fear
Undermine	to attack or weaken indirectly, subvert
Vivify	to bring to life, enliven

NOW YOU TRY

Fill in the blanks in the following sentences by using each of the words in the following word bank:

Adroit	Aloof	Arbitrary	Augment	Blatant
Drivel	Enhance	Ensconced	Gratis	Hoary
Inconspicuous	Infamous	Malinger	Munificent	Pallid
Placid	Posterity	Profanity	Recant	Skeptical
Subversive	Terse	Trepidation	Undermine	Vivify

1. The applicant was not chosen for the new position because his interview was filled with a lot of useless _____.
2. After forgetting the table's appetizer, the server offered to bring them a desert _____.
3. The doctor took special note of the patient's _____ complexion when examining her after surgery.
4. His skill with his hands made him very _____ at fixing things around the house.
5. Everyone in the town celebrated the death of the _____ dictator.
6. The zookeeper was shocked when the normally _____ goat began displaying rather aggressive behavior.
7. She shook in _____ at the thought of going sky diving because she had a paralyzing fear of heights.
8. An _____ student was chosen by the teacher to go and get the forms from the office.
9. After her plan for dinner with friends fell through, she decided to spend the evening _____ in a chair with a good book.
10. The man was well-known at the food bank for being very charitable and _____.
11. The lawyer struggled to get any information from the witness because of their _____ responses.
12. Writing in a journal is a great way to document your life for _____.
13. Although at first the man seemed _____, once the party got started he was fun and energetic.
14. The judge was _____ of the defendant's guilt, but could not rule against the jury's decision.
15. The gymnast hoped to _____ her competition by hiding the remainder of the hand chalk.
16. Hoping to remain _____, the private detective followed his mark at a distance of thirty feet.
17. The teacher informed her students that they could _____ their presentations by using visual aids.

18. Samantha worked to _____ her bank account by reserving 10 percent of her income for savings each week.
19. When he discovered that his car had been towed, the man angrily let loose a stream of _____.
20. Despite her grandfather's age, the girl was offended when her friend called him a _____ old man.
21. After learning that she would not be fired after all, Natalie decided to _____ the rude statements she had made about her boss.
22. When people started falling asleep, the party planner decided to start playing music to _____ the remaining guests.
23. The principal was shocked by the student's _____ disregard for the rules when they spray painted the hallway green.
24. The tyrant chose to censor all media in the country to stop _____ information from being distributed.
25. When Derik called in sick, the manager had a feeling he was simply choosing to _____ rather than complete his paperwork.

ANSWERS

1. Drivel
2. Gratis
3. Pallid
4. Adroit
5. Infamous
6. Placid
7. Trepidation
8. Arbitrary
9. Ensconced
10. Munificent
11. Terse
12. Posterity
13. Aloof
14. Skeptical
15. Undermine
16. Inconspicuous
17. Enhance
18. Augment
19. Profanity
20. Hoary
21. Recant
22. Vivify
23. Blatant
24. Subversive
25. Malinger

VOCABULARY LIST #20

Antagonism	hostility, opposition
Atrophy	waste away, weaken
Auspicious	favorable, fortunate, prosperous
Candor	sincere, candid, open
Chary	cautious, timid
Commandeer	to take control of by force
Covert	undercover
Deteriorate	disintegrate, worsen, wear away
Drawl	slow, slurred speech
Exasperated	irritated, annoyed
Gravity	weightiness, seriousness
Heed	take note of, listen to, hear
Impoverished	in poverty, poor, destitute
Infer	conclude by logical reasoning
Languid	listless, tired, weak
Mortality	subject to death
Objective	goal; unbiased
Pernicious	hurtful, ruinous, wicked
Polemical	controversial, argumentative
Precedent	a prior example, pattern, decision
Quagmire	marsh, bog
Serrated	jagged
Strut	pompous walk, swagger
Subtle	difficult to perceive, not obvious
Truncate	cut off, cut short

NOW YOU TRY

List an antonym for the following words:

1. Antagonism   _____

2. Atrophy   _____

3. Auspicious   _____

4. Candor   _____

5. Chary   _____

6. Commandeer   _____

7. Covert   _____

8. Deteriorate   _____

9. Drawl   _____

10. Exasperated   _____

11. Gravity   _____

12. Heed   _____

13. Impoverished   _____

14. Infer   _____

15. Languid   _____

16. Mortality   _____

17. Objective   _____

18. Pernicious   _____

19. Polemical   _____

20. Precedent   _____

21. Quagmire   _____

22. Serrated   _____

23. Strut   _____

24. Subtle   _____

25. Truncate   _____

ANSWERS

1. Supporter
2. Strengthen
3. Ominous
4. Subversive
5. Forceful
6. Request
7. Overt
8. Construct
9. Eloquent
10. Soothed
11. Insignificance
12. Ignore
13. Affluent
14. Misunderstand
15. Energetic
16. Immortality
17. Subjective
18. Angelic
19. Agreeable
20. Subsequent
21. Desert
22. Smooth
23. Modest
24. Obvious
25. Elongate

VOCABULARY LIST #21

Condone	overlook, allow, not prevent
Egress	exit, emerge, go out
Flamboyant	ostentatious, conspicuous, showy
Garnish	decorative top, adornment
Immutable	unchanging, ageless
Incipient	beginning, in initial stages
Inevitable	unavoidable
Intricate	ornate, detailed, complex
Lax	easygoing, lenient
Maladroit	clumsy
Fallacious	false, not logical
Glacial	cold, hostile
Illuminate	to bring light, brighten, clarify
Inexorable	immovable, relentless, unyielding
Legion	military unit; large number
Marshal	highest-ranking officer, combine, gather
Moratorium	temporary pause or halt
Pariah	social outcast
Perfunctory	indifferent, disinterested, cursory
Prerogative	right or privilege
Rebuttal	argument against; denial
Tome	large, heavy, difficult book
Unwitting	accidental, not purposely, unconscious
Vapid	lifeless, dull, boring
Voluminous	large, expansive

NOW YOU TRY

Determine whether the underlined word is used correctly (C) or incorrectly (I) in the sentence.

C I 1. Rather than nag him incessantly, she decided to <u>condone</u> her child's behavior while company was present.

C I 2. Instead of waiting in the hall as instructed, the intern chose to <u>egress</u> the meeting room.

C I 3. The beat up, old car was so <u>flamboyant</u> that it was hard to spot in a crowd.

C I 4. The baker <u>garnished</u> the cupcake with sprinkles to add color and flare to its presentation.

C I 5. It is an <u>immutable</u> truth that the sun is the center of the galaxy, and not the earth.

C I 6. Because he waited so long to go to the doctor, his cold was <u>incipient</u>.

C I 7. When Jenna did not turn in her final project, she knew she would <u>inevitably</u> fail her class.

C I 8. The room was <u>intricately</u> decorated with a spiral pattern painted on the walls, and a number of ornate draperies hanging from the ceiling.

C I 9. Students loved the teacher for his <u>lax</u> and easygoing attitude about homework.

C I 10. She quickly and beautifully hemmed the skirt, displaying her <u>maladroit</u> technique.

C I 11. The student's <u>fallacious</u> argument won the debate for her team.

C I 12. When the manager told Sam that he was being laid off, his attitude became <u>glacial</u> and he slammed the door on his way out of the office.

C I 13. Because she did not want her competitors to find the clue, Sally <u>illuminated</u> it by hiding it behind a tree.

C I 14. After she learned that her mother was sick, Jane was <u>inexorable</u> in her resolve to go and visit her.

C I 15. At one time, the Roman <u>legion</u> was the most powerful force in the world.

C I 16. Everyone gave deference to the <u>Marshal</u> when he spoke.

C I 17. Due to the immediate need for corn, Congress ordered a <u>moratorium</u> on planting corn.

C I 18. Antony feared that if he did not go to his friend's party he would be viewed as a <u>pariah</u>.

C I 19. The teacher was pleased with the student's <u>perfunctory</u> responses. She could tell that they were genuinely interested in the subject of their essay.

C I 20. The mayor decided to exercise his <u>prerogative</u> and pass the law without the committee's approval.

C I 21. After the evidence was presented by the plaintiff, the defense was given a chance at <u>rebuttal</u>.

C I 22. One could not help but be impressed by the extensive <u>tome</u> collection – most of the books were over 1000 pages long.

C I 23. The politician's <u>unwitting</u> support of his opponent's position became his ultimate downfall in the race.

C I 24. Many students felt that the teacher was <u>vapid</u> and boring. They rarely stayed awake through the class.

C I 25. Because of the excessive number of people in the hallway, it felt <u>voluminous</u> and cramped.

ANSWERS

1. C
2. I
3. I
4. C
5. C
6. I
7. C
8. C
9. C
10. I
11. I
12. C
13. I
14. C
15. C
16. C
17. I
18. C
19. I
20. C
21. C
22. C
23. C
24. C
25. I

VOCABULARY LIST #22

Alleviate	lessen the severity, mitigate
Amass	accumulate
Apprehensive	uneasy, worried, afraid
Benign	kind, gentle; not cancerous
Circumscribe	encircle, limit, confine
Collude	conspire, plot (with evil intent)
Deride	ridicule, jeer at, taunt
Discern	distinguish, perceive
Ebullient	full of enthusiasm and excitement, cheerful
Flippant	light-minded, joking, disrespectful
Lobbyist	one who argues for or promotes an idea
Menagerie	collection of animals; varied group of people
Mundane	worldly, human, ordinary
Parasite	an organism which lives off of others
Portent	sign, omen, foreshadowing
Precept	guiding principle
Quaff	drink copiously, heartily
Quaint	picturesque
Receptacle	bin, container
Sardonic	mocking, spiteful, hurtful
Tardy	late
Turpitude	depravity, vile, shameful
Ubiquitous	existing everywhere simultaneously
Unfetter	remove bonds from, set free
Urbane	suave, elegant, sophisticated

NOW YOU TRY

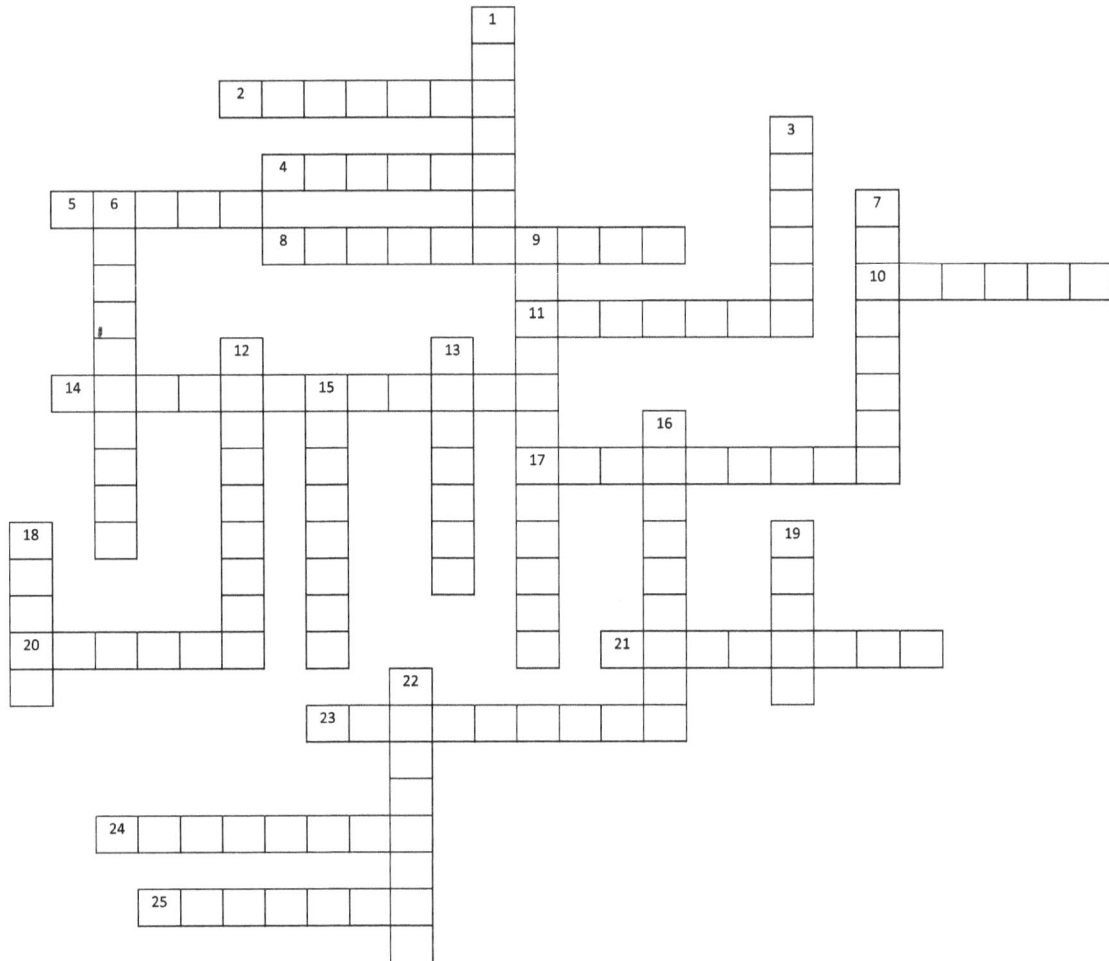

Across

2. worldly, human, ordinary
4. suave, elegant, sophisticated
5. drink copiously, heartily
8. bin, container
10. kind, gentle; not cancerous
11. sign, omen, foreshadowing
14. encircle, limit, confine
17. full of enthusiasm and excitement, cheerful
20. ridicule, jeer at, taunt
21. an organism which lives off of others
23. collection of animals, variety
24. light-minded, joking, disrespectful
25. conspire, plot (with evil intent)

Down

1. guiding principle
3. picturesque
6. existing everywhere simultaneously
7. one who argues for an idea
9. uneasy, worried, afraid
12. depravity, vile, shameful
13. distinguish, perceive
15. mocking, spiteful, hurtful
16. lessen the severity, mitigate
18. late
19. accumulate
22. remove bonds from, set free

ANSWERS

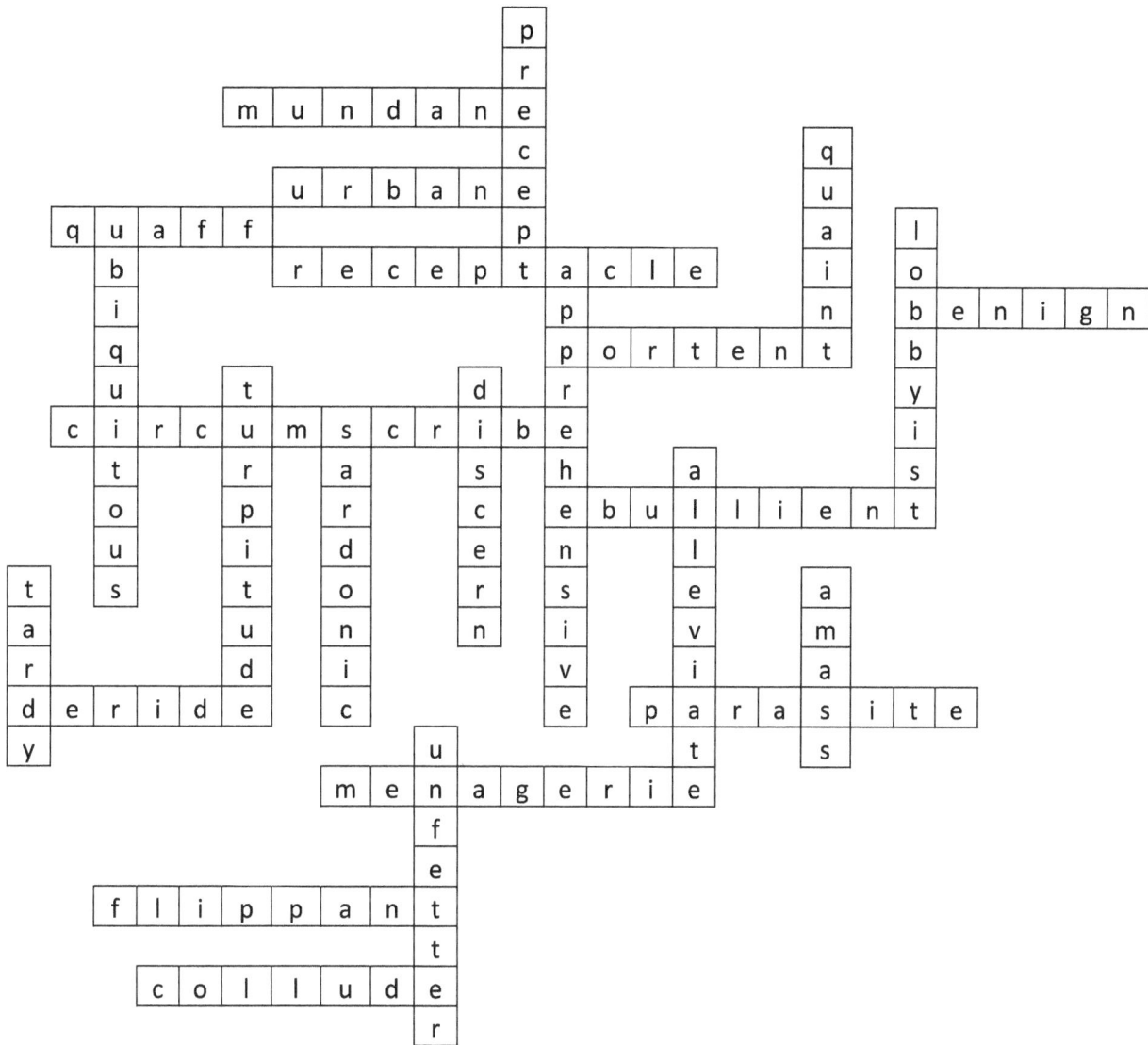

VOCABULARY LIST #23

Abstruse	incomprehensible, obscure, confusing
Adamant	unyielding, determined, forceful
Alacrity	liveliness, enthusiasm, willingness
Banal	trite, unoriginal, boring
Bolster	support
Callow	immature, inexperienced
Clandestine	concealed, private, stealthy, covert
Denounce	condemn, renounce, openly oppose
Dynamic	forceful, energetic, vibrant
Effigy	crude represent or model of a person
Omnipotent	all-powerful
Patronize	demean, condescend to, criticize
Prosaic	dull, unimaginative, not creative
Quarry	stone mine, hunted game
Repudiate	reject, disown, condemn
Sequester	isolate, separate
Stoic	steadfast, unemotional, passionless
Tentative	shy, uncertain
Transcribe	copy, write
Unpalatable	inedible; unacceptable
Upbraid	reprimand
Upshot	result, outcome, gist
Utilitarian	useful
Vociferous	noisy
Wax	extend, enlarge, increase, grow

NOW YOU TRY

Using the word bank, fill in the blanks in the following sentences:

Abstruse	Adamant	Alacrity	Banal	Bolster
Callow	Clandestine	Denounced	Dynamic	Effigy
Omnipotent	Patronize	Prosaic	Quarry	Repudiate
Sequester	Stoic	Tentative	Transcribe	Unpalatable
Upbraid	Upshot	Utilitarian	Vociferous	Wax

1. Although he wouldn't admit it, everyone could see that the boater was _____ because he didn't even bring a life preserver or GPS.
2. Jane _____ the manager's proposal to extend the work day until 7 o'clock.
3. He was _____ that no one would go home until the last forms had been filed and completed.
4. The mob was so angry with the criminal that they burned him in _____ outside the courthouse.
5. The man's performance was so _____ that most of the audience left halfway through.
6. After the prison fight started, the guards decided to _____ the culprits and punish them separately.
7. When she presented her work to the connoisseur, she was heartbroken when he called it _____ and unimpressive.
8. The professor assured the class that there wouldn't be any _____ information on the next exam.
9. The critic sent the food back to the kitchen and called it _____ because it still had crab shells in it.
10. The negotiators proposed a _____ solution to the problem, hoping that both parties would accept it.
11. The lawyer begged his client not to _____ the jury: they needed to make a good impression.
12. After the defense witness was examined, the plaintiff was given a chance to _____ his testimony.
13. The teacher was going to repeat himself, but the class insisted that they got the _____ of what he had said.
14. After weeks of heavy weight lifting, the man's muscles finally began to _____ stronger.
15. The manager chose the applicant for the job because of their _____ and optimism in the interview.
16. The _____ crowd would not be quieted by the ushers.
17. After the house burned down, the mother was so relieved that her children were safe that she did not _____ them for playing with matches for several days.

18. The comedian was a favorite in Las Vegas because he was so _____ and lively.
19. In order to ensure that nothing was forgotten, they hired a stenographer to _____ everything they said.
20. The judge remained _____ throughout the trial, not giving any hint to his true opinion.
21. Although the man's invention was _____, the company would not produce it because it did not look attractive.
22. Samantha complimented her sister profusely, wanting to _____ her confidence.
23. Jonathan did not want to admit his surprise because he wanted the employees to believe he was _____.
24. The entire _____ operation was blown when the officer's true identity was revealed.
25. After trailing the deer all day, the hunter smiled as he closed in on his _____.

ANSWERS

1. Callow
2. Denounced
3. Adamant
4. Effigy
5. Banal
6. Sequester
7. Prosaic
8. Abstruse
9. Unpalatable
10. Tentative
11. Patronize
12. Repudiate
13. Upshot
14. Wax
15. Alacrity
16. Vociferous
17. Upbraid
18. Dynamic
19. Transcribe
20. Stoic
21. Utilitarian
22. Bolster
23. Omnipotent
24. Clandestine
25. Quarry

VOCABULARY LIST #24

Ambivalence	unclear, ambiguous, uncertain
Amity	friendship
Archaic	ancient, antiquated, obsolete
Byline	line which identifies the author of an article
Cower	recoil, crouch, shrink back in fear or shame
Detrimental	damaging
Eclectic	random, from many sources
Exposition	unveiling, thorough explanation
Genre	category
Ineffable	inexpressible, sacred
Insurgent	rebel
Lofty	high up; superior; arrogant
Misrepresentation	to present so as to deceive or confuse
Parry	dodge, evade, ward off
Plaudit	enthusiastic approval or praise
Preclude	prevent
Proclivity	natural inclination, tendency
Rant	long, angry speech
Resonant	powerful, resounding, echoing
Stoke	supply, stir up, strengthen
Stringent	strict, constraining
Tangent	almost irrelevant, off the main subject
Torpor	apathetic, sluggish, lethargic
Vacillate	be indecisive, waver
Virulent	noxious, dangerous

NOW YOU TRY

Match the word with its definition.

1. Ambivalence	a. recoil, crouch, shrink back in fear or shame
2. Amity	b. damaging
3. Archaic	c. enthusiastic approval or praise
4. Byline	d. prevent
5. Cower	e. friendship
6. Detrimental	f. be indecisive, waver
7. Eclectic	g. rebel
8. Exposition	h. unveiling, thorough explanation
9. Genre	i. strict, constraining
10. Ineffable	j. powerful, resounding, echoing
11. Insurgent	k. ancient, antiquated, obsolete
12. Lofty	l. noxious, dangerous
13. Misrepresentation	m. apathetic, sluggish, lethargic
14. Parry	n. natural inclination, tendency
15. Plaudit	o. random, from many sources
16. Preclude	p. line which identifies the author of an article
17. Proclivity	q. almost irrelevant, off the main subject
18. Rant	r. long, angry speech
19. Resonant	s. supply, stir up, strengthen
20. Stoke	t. inexpressible, sacred
21. Stringent	u. to present so as to deceive or confuse
22. Tangent	v. category
23. Torpor	w. dodge, evade, ward off
24. Vacillate	x. unclear, ambiguous, uncertain
25. Virulent	y. high up; superior; arrogant

ANSWERS

1. x
2. e
3. k
4. p
5. a
6. b
7. o
8. h
9. v
10. t
11. g
12. y
13. u
14. w
15. c
16. d
17. n
18. r
19. j
20. s
21. i
22. q
23. m
24. f
25. l

📖 *Sentence Completion Sample Test Questions*

1. Because Sam's boss was so _____ about the job being finished correctly, Sam asked him to repeat himself because his initial instructions were rather _____.

   A) Lax, coherent
   B) Obstinate, lucid
   C) Uncertain, obscure
   D) Resolute, eloquent
   E) Adamant, ambivalent

The correct answer is E:) Adamant, ambivalent. It is unlikely that a boss would be lax or uncertain about wanting a job finished correctly. It is more likely that he would be resolute or adamant. Considering the second blank, this means that it will be filled with either eloquent or ambivalent. If his instructions were eloquent, they would not need to be repeated, so the correct answer must be E.

2. After not practicing medicine for many years, the doctor's techniques were _____ and many of the other doctors were _____ that he was qualified for the position.

   A) Modernized, cynical
   B) Archaic, skeptical
   C) Subversive, uncertain
   D) Antiquated, certain
   E) Terse, polemical

The correct answer is B:) Archaic, skeptical. If the doctor had not practiced for many years, his techniques would not be modernized. A doctor's techniques would also not be subversive as this would indicate the doctor was seditious. It also wouldn't make sense to say that the techniques were terse, as this refers to speech. This leaves options B and D; i.e., the techniques could be either archaic or antiquated. Looking at the second blank, this leaves the options of either skeptical (answer B) or certain (answer A). If the techniques were up-to-date then the other doctor's would have no reason to question his qualifications; however, he has not practiced for many years. Therefore, the correct answer must be B.

3. The doctor was pleased to inform the patient that he could prescribe a _____ that would help his skin condition and ensure his _____ if he would apply it three times a day.

    A) Liniment, longevity
    B) Analgesic, permanence
    C) Contaminant, robustness
    D) Panacea, mortality
    E) Toxin, salubriousness

The correct answer is A:) Liniment, longevity. A doctor would not prescribe a toxin or a contaminant as either one is considered a dangerous substance. This leaves option A, a liniment or soothing lotion; option B, an analgesic or pain reliever; and option D, a panacea or cure-all. Because it is a skin condition that is involved, liniment and panacea are more likely than analgesic. Looking at the second blank, this leaves the options longevity and mortality. It makes more sense for a doctor to wish to ensure longevity (long-life) than their mortality (that they are subject to death). This makes the correct answer A.

4. The volunteer was so _____ that the crowd could feel with _____ that he cared about the cause.

    A) Vigorous, ambivalence
    B) Euphonious, trepidation
    C) Vivacious, certitude
    D) Lethargic, conviction
    E) Negligent, vehemence

The correct answer is C:) Vivacious, certitude. Answer A indicates that the crowd is unsure about the volunteer's feelings because of their vigorous manner. If the volunteer were vigorous then the crowd would not be unsure. Answer B doesn't make sense. Trepidation is synonymous with fear, and is out of place in the sentence. Answer D indicates that the crowd is sure the volunteer cares because he is tired and slow. This does not make sense, so answer D cannot be correct. Answer E doesn't make sense because vehemence does not fit in the sentence. Therefore, the correct answer is C.

5. The duke was _____ to discover that after he had paid 100 thousand dollars in advance, the decorator had disappeared and left the walls _____.

    A) Pertinent, lavish
    B) Livid, austere
    C) Irate, germane
    D) Jaded, plain
    E) Languid, ascetic

The correct answer is B:) Livid, austere. If the decorator has disappeared with the duke's money, it is unlikely that he will be languid. Also, pertinent does not fit in the sentence; therefore, answers A and E cannot be correct. Answer D cannot be correct because the duke would also not be jaded, which means dull or worn out. This leaves answer choices B and C; i.e., the duke was either livid or irate, either of which fits in the context.

Considering the second blank, this leaves the options austere (answer B) and germane (answer C). Germane, meaning relevant, does not make sense in the context of the question. Therefore, answer B is the correct option.

6. The woman was so _____ at making quilts that people would come from miles around to obtain one of her _____ masterpieces.

    A) Inept, lavish
    B) Maladroit, quaint
    C) Flamboyant, urbane
    D) Adept, banal
    E) Adroit, intricate

The correct answer is E:) Adroit, intricate. For people to come from miles around, the quilts must be well made. This makes answer D, adept, and answer E, adroit, the most likely options. Intricate makes more sense in the context of the sentence. The correct answer choice is E.

7. The _____ chef did not remember to strain the shells out of the sauce. As a result, the critic announced that it was _____, and he refused to eat it.

   A) Dynamic, noxious
   B) Stoic, archaic
   C) Naïve, hoary
   D) Callow, unpalatable
   E) Exasperated, delicious

The correct answer is D:) Callow, unpalatable. If the chef forgot a step in preparing the food, this indicates that he is inexperienced. This makes answers C and D the most likely. Looking at the second blank in the sentence, this leaves hoary and unpalatable as an option. In the context of the question unpalatable, or inedible, makes the most sense. Therefore, the correct option is answer D.

8. When the paper arrived each week, the mother _____ scanned the _____ to see if any of the articles were written by her daughter.

   A) Breathlessly, legend
   B) Languidly, enigma
   C) Diffidently, pages
   D) Eagerly, bylines
   E) Unwittingly, headlines

The correct answer is D:) Eagerly, bylines. The mother who is looking to see if her daughter wrote any of the articles would be excited and proud. She would not be languid (answer B), diffident (answer C), or unwitting (answer E). Each of these options can therefore be eliminated.

Moving to the second answer blank, papers have pages, bylines, and headlines; however, they do not have legends or enigmas. This further eliminates answer A, leaving D as the only possible answer. Answer D makes perfect sense because the mother would be eager, and by scanning the bylines she would quickly determine the author of each article.

9. In order to keep the streets looking nice, the officer worked tirelessly to
    _____ the _____ homeless people into the homeless shelter.

    A) Isolate, covert
    B) Sequester, impoverished
    C) Truncate, auspicious
    D) Extol, prodigious
    E) Goad, intrepid

The correct answer is B:) Sequester, impoverished. First consider the first answer blank. It does not make sense for an officer to truncate, or cut short, the homeless people. Therefore answer C can be eliminated. It is also unlikely that he would goad, or taunt, them if he is seeking their cooperation, so answer E can be eliminated.

Looking at the second answer blank, it is unlikely that homeless people would be described as prodigious. It also doesn't make sense that the officer would "extol the prodigious homeless people into the homeless shelter." Praising them would not result in their movement to the shelter.

This leaves answer choices A and B as possibilities, both of which make sense because the streets would stay nice if the homeless people were sequestered or isolated (i.e., moved) to the shelter. Answer A can be eliminated because if the people were covert then it wouldn't be necessary to move them. However, homeless people can be described as impoverished; therefore, the correct answer is B.

10. Many voters would not _____ the candidate because his campaign strategy
    primarily involved a series of harsh _____ against his opponent, rather
    than stating his position.

    A) Heed, diatribes
    B) Sanction, idiosyncrasies
    C) Enfranchise, usurpations
    D) Regard, misnomers
    E) Oust, platitudes

The correct answer is A:) Heed, diatribes. Examining the first answer blank, only answer C can be eliminated. Candidates do not need to be given the right to vote, they simply need people to vote for them. However, any of the other options are possible actions voters could take. Considering the second answer blank, however, it would not make sense to say that the candidate made idiosyncrasies, usurpations, or misnomers about his opponent. This leaves only options A or E as possibilities.

Answer A indicates that the voters will not listen to the candidate because he simply criticizes his opponent. Answer E indicates that they will not reject him because he is boring. Of the two, answer A is the more likely scenario.

11. The manager _____ the newest employee because her work was
     _____.

    A) Fired, exemplary
    B) Exalted, prodigal
    C) Extolled, irreproachable
    D) Commended, torpid
    E) Ousted, profound

The correct answer is C:) Extolled, irreproachable. For this sentence, it is impossible to determine if the manager is pleased or upset. Therefore, to answer you must consider each pair of words as they fit into the blank. The manager would not fire an exemplary employee, they would be happy with their work. Further, they would not exalt a prodigal employee, they would criticize their wastefulness. This eliminates options A and B.

The manager also would not commend a torpid employee, they would encourage them to be more energetic. It is also unlikely that they would oust, or get rid of, a profound employee. This leaves only option C as a possibility. It would make sense for the manager to extol, or praise, an employee for irreproachable, or flawless work. Therefore, the correct answer is C.

12. There was often a long _____ at the second checkout stand because the
     clerk was more _____ and good-natured than the others.

    A) Queue, personable
    B) Delay, adroit
    C) Hiatus, brusque
    D) Vacancy, choleric
    E) Wait, poised

The correct answer is A:) Queue, personable. Looking at the second blank, answers C and D can be eliminated because it is not logical to describe the clerk as both good-natured and brusque or choleric. The rest of the options can be evaluated based on how the pairs of words fit in the sentence.

Considering answer B, there would not be a delay at the checkout stand if the clerk was adroit. Rather, she would be able to move people through quickly. Answer E is also illogical because the clerk being poised would not have any effect on the wait in the line.

This leaves answer A as the correct option. It does make sense to say that there is a longer line of people at the checkout stand because the clerk is friendly. More people would want to go through that line.

13. Despite her kind _____, Sally often _____ hurt her sister's feelings by being too judgmental.

    A) Personality, indifferently
    B) Inclinations, infallibly
    C) Depravity, accidentally
    D) Complacency, intentionally
    E) Intentions, inadvertently

The correct answer is E:) Intentions, inadvertently. Answer C can be eliminated because "kind depravity" does not make sense. The two words have opposite meanings. Answers A, B, and D can be eliminated because if Sally is kind (as is indicated in the first half of the sentence) then she would not hurt her sister's feelings on purpose. Therefore, answer E, which indicates that she accidentally hurts her sister's feelings, is correct.

14. Gold is often used in making jewelry because it is _____ and easy to form. It also holds its color and is _____ rather than transparent like some substances.

    A) Malleable, opaque
    B) Green, vibrant
    C) Transparent, brittle
    D) Pervasive, weighty
    E) Stolid, immutable

The correct answer is A:) Malleable, opaque. Gold is used in jewelry because it is easy to form (as the passage indicates). This is the definition of the word malleable. Furthermore, something that is "not transparent" is referred to as opaque. Therefore, the correct answer is A.

15. While the queen adored the decorations, and thought they were classic and _____, the king found them _____ and ordered her to change them.

    A) Ornate, urbane
    B) Timeless, refined
    C) Strident, polemical
    D) Immutable, garish
    E) Hoary, austere

The correct answer is D:) Immutable, garish. The queen would not adore the decorations if they were strident or hoary, so answers C and E can be eliminated. Furthermore, the king would not dislike the decorations if they were urbane or refined, so answers A and B can be eliminated. Therefore, D is the correct answer.

16. After carefully _____ the evidence, the judge was _____ that it was relevant to the case, and decided that it was not admissible.

    A) Augmenting, hesitant
    B) Examining, certain
    C) Scrutinizing, dubious
    D) Perusing, assured
    E) Razing, convinced

The correct answer is C:) Scrutinizing, dubious. Looking at the first answer blank, it would not make sense to augment or raze evidence in a trial. Because of this, answers A and E can be eliminated. Considering the second answer blank, the judge would not deem the evidence inadmissible if he were assured or certain that it was relevant, therefore answers B and D can be eliminated. Therefore, answer C is the correct answer.

17. The tired hikers were rewarded after their long, _____ climb by a beautiful view of a _____ lake.

    A) Modest, attractive
    B) Relaxed, glacial
    C) Perfunctory, infamous
    D) Grim, hoary
    E) Arduous, pristine

The correct answer is E:) Arduous, pristine. Considering the first answer blank, it would not make sense to describe the long hike as modest, relaxed, or perfunctory, so answers A, B, and C can be eliminated. Looking at the remaining options for the second blank, it would be illogical to describe the lake as both beautiful and hoary. Therefore, the correct answer must be E.

18. Although the two had always had _____ for each other, her _____ comment threatened to end their friendship.

    A) Adoration, intrepid
    B) Amity, invidious
    C) Rancor, pretentious
    D) Goodwill, despondent
    E) Malice, carping

The correct answer is B:) Amity, invidious. Because the sentence is describing two friends, answers C and E can be eliminated. Friends would not have rancor or malice for each other. Considering the options for the second blank, it is unlikely that an intrepid or despondent comment would ruin their friendship, so answers A and D can be eliminated. This leaves B as the correct answer. This is logical because it indicates that despite their kindness (amity) the hurtful, or invidious, comment threatened their friendship.

19. Her resolve to stick to her diet began to _____ as the hostess set out a fresh, homemade chocolate cake.

    A) Absolve
    B) Fortify
    C) Augment
    D) Attenuate
    E) Rancor

The correct answer is D:) Attenuate. It is most likely that it would become more difficult to diet as the dessert was presented. Therefore the most logical option is answer D, attenuate or weaken. It would not make sense that it would be fortified or augmented because both of these options indicate a strengthening of her resolve. The options absolve and rancor do not make any sense in the context of the sentence.

20. The politician was faced with quite a _____: by sticking to his platform he would _____ a large portion of voters.

    A) Bulwark, confuse
    B) Predicament, appeal to
    C) Lithe, disillusion
    D) Quandary, estrange
    E) Picayune, subterfuge

The correct answer is D:) Quandary, estrange. Answers C and E can be eliminated because you cannot be faced with "a" lithe or picayune because they are both adjectives, not nouns. Answer A can be eliminated because it does not make sense to say the politician was faced with a bulwark, or wall. This leaves options B and D.

Option B indicates that the politician faces a dilemma because his platform appeals to voters. This option does not make sense because it does not present a dilemma. Option D indicates that the politician faces a dilemma because voters would disagree with his platform. Therefore, option D is the correct answer.

21. The manager thought that it was very _____ of the applicant to quit his old job before he had officially hired him.

    A) Presumptuous
    B) Cynical
    C) Obsequious
    D) Pragmatic
    E) Ambiguous

The correct answer is A:) Presumptuous. Answer B can be eliminated because it is not cynical of the applicant to quit their job; rather, it would be cynical if they did not quit their job for long after a positive interview. Answer D can be eliminated because it is not pragmatic, or logical, to quit one job before receiving any assurance of getting another. Answer E can be eliminated because it is also not ambiguous; rather, it sends the clear message that the applicant expects to get the job. Finally, answer C can be eliminated because it isn't brown-nosing if the applicant doesn't do things which benefit the manager. Therefore, the correct answer is A. It is presumptuous, or assuming, if the applicant is so certain that he will get the job.

22. It is the editor's job to eliminate _____ information, and to ensure that the writing is as _____ as possible.

    A) Paramount, obtuse
    B) Irrelevant, ambivalent
    C) Extraneous, concise
    D) Circuitous, cryptic
    E) Imperative, succinct

The correct answer is C:) Extraneous, concise. Examining the first answer choice, answers A and E can be eliminated because an editor would not want to eliminate important information. Considering the second answer choice, the editor would not want to make the writing confusing, so answer B, ambivalent, and answer C, cryptic, can be eliminated. This makes answer C the correct answer.

23. Most of the students were confused by the professor's _____ lectures, and bored by his _____ presentation skills.

    A) Austere, incoherent
    B) Cantankerous, impromptu
    C) Unequivocal, preeminent
    D) Explicit, concise
    E) Arcane, lackluster

The correct answer is E:) Arcane, lackluster. The students would not be confused by the lectures if they were austere (plain), unequivocal (clear), or explicit. Therefore, options A, C, and D can be eliminated. Looking at the second answer blank, it makes more sense that the students would be bored by lackluster presentation skills than by impromptu presentation skills (which has an entirely different meaning). Therefore, the correct answer is E.

24. When seen in debate, the two candidates starkly contrasted each other. The first gave a speech that was _____, and much of the audience was put to sleep. The other spoke with _____ and had them standing on their feet.

    A) Trite, turpitude
    B) Banal, alacrity
    C) Flippant, antagonism
    D) Ambiguous, a drawl
    E) Vivacious, rancor

The correct answer is B:) Banal, alacrity. Looking at the first answer blank, the audience would not necessarily be put to sleep if the speech were flippant, ambiguous, or vivacious. However, they would certainly be put to sleep if it were banal or trite. Looking at the second answer blank, it is possible that the crowd were on their feet with anger if the candidate spoke with turpitude; however, it is more logical to say that the two candidates were in contrast if the crowd was on their feet with excitement. Therefore, answer B is the correct answer.

25. When the intern spelled her name wrong, the manager felt that it was such a(n) _____ mistake that it was _____ that he fire her immediately.

    A) Inexcusable, parsimonious
    B) Myopic, pervasive
    C) Boorish, insensitive
    D) Egregious, expedient
    E) Obscure, supercilious

The correct answer is D:) Egregious, expedient. Considering the first answer blank, it is most likely that the mistake would be described as either inexcusable or egregious because it is such an obvious and simple mistake. Therefore, the answer is most likely A or D. Answer A can be eliminated because it would not be parsimonious for him to fire her. Therefore, the correct answer is D.

26. Everyone knew that the rumbling clouds were a _____ of the coming storm; however, no one predicted that the lightning would result in a(n) _____ that would destroy the whole city.

    A) Omen, tsunami
    B) Beneficiary, euphony
    C) Presage, analgesic
    D) Portent, conflagration
    E) Paramount, inferno

The correct answer is D:) Portent, conflagration. Consider the second answer blank, a lightning would not cause a tsunami, euphony, or analgesic, so options A, B and C can be eliminated. Answer E can be eliminated because it doesn't make sense to say that the clouds were a paramount of the coming storm. This leaves answer D which logically indicates that the clouds were an omen, and that the lightning caused a fire. Therefore the correct answer is D.

27. The entire kitchen staff was intimidated by the new chef's _____ upon discovering that the kitchen supplies were _____ and not suitable for use.

    A) Rant, utilitarian
    B) Drawl, deteriorating
    C) Tirade, defunct
    D) Candor, functional
    E) Anger, polemical

The correct answer is C:) Tirade, defunct. Answers B and D can be eliminated because it does not make sense to say that the staff were intimidated by the chef's candor or drawl. Answer A can be eliminated because utilitarian supplies would be suitable for use. Answer E can be eliminated because polemical does not fit in the context of the sentence. Therefore, the correct answer is C.

28. After graduating with her law degree, Sally was eager to _____ her skills in the courtroom, and took on many cases _____ in order to attract more clients quickly.

   A) Enhance, gratis
   B) Degrade, arbitrarily
   C) Augment, dilatorily
   D) Attenuate, subversively
   E) Display, covertly

The correct answer is A:) Enhance, gratis. Based on the first answer blank, options B and D can be eliminated because she wouldn't want to degrade or attenuate her skills in the courtroom. Based on the second answer blank, answer E can be eliminated because it would not help her gain more clients if she takes some on covertly. Answer C can be eliminated because if she takes on cases dilatorily, or slowly, then she would not gain new clients quickly. Therefore answer A is the correct answer.

29. The judge would not allow the jury to _____ the courtroom until the defense was given a fair chance at a _____ of the plaintiff's witness.

   A) Upshot, negation
   B) Traverse, moratorium
   C) Enter, denial
   D) Emerge from, condone
   E) Egress, rebuttal

The correct answer is E:) Egress, rebuttal. Based on the second answer blank, options B and D can be eliminated because the defense would not want to condone or have a moratorium of the plaintiff's witness. Option A can be eliminated because "upshot" does not make sense in the context of the sentence. Answer C can be eliminated because it would not make sense for the judge to prevent the jury from entering the courtroom during testimony. Therefore, the correct answer is E.

30. The name of Benedict Arnold lives in _____ because of his _____ during the Revolutionary War.

    A) Disdain, valor
    B) Infamy, perfidy
    C) Serendipity, treachery
    D) Renown, deceit
    E) Ignominy, gallantry

The correct answer is B:) Infamy, perfidy. Answer A can be eliminated because it would not make sense for a person to be disdained for their valor during war. Answer C can be eliminated because it would be illogical to think of treachery as serendipitous. Answer D can be eliminated because a person would not have renown or honor if they had acted deceitfully. Answer E can be eliminated because a person would not be ignominious if they had acted gallantly. Therefore, answer B is the correct answer.

31. Because she felt that her figure was becoming increasingly _____, Anabeth decided that she would _____ from/in desserts for the next two months.

    A) Thin, refrain
    B) Plump, indulge
    C) Rotund, abstain
    D) Reedy, refrain
    E) Stolid, obviate

The correct answer is C:) Rotund, abstain. Answer E can be eliminated because it does not make sense to describe a figure as stolid. Answer A can be eliminated because if she considers herself thin there is no need to make a special effort to refrain from deserts. Similarly, if she feels reedy, she is more likely to consume more desserts than avoid them. This leaves answers B and C. Answer B can be eliminated because if she feels plump she will not want to indulge in desserts. Therefore, the correct answer is C.

32. The jury was _____ by the witness's testimony because it contradicted the testimony of another witness. They knew that one of the two must have committed _____, because they could not both be telling the truth.

   A) Bristled, larceny
   B) Expedited, arson
   C) Perplexed, burglary
   D) Befuddled, perjury
   E) Confounded, murder

The correct answer is D:) Befuddled, perjury. Lying under oath is referred to as perjury. This means that answer D must be the correct answer because it is the only option that identifies the correct crime.

33. Although the lawyer was certain that his client was guilty of (a) _____ of crimes, he had to defend him regardless because it was his job to _____ him.

   A) Myriad, advocate
   B) Countless, condemn
   C) Plethora, repudiate
   D) Modicum, undermine
   E) No number, defend

The correct answer is A:) Myriad, advocate. Considering the answers which fit the first blank, the lawyer would not be conflicted about defending the client if they were innocent, so answers D and E can be eliminated. Looking at the second blank, it is the job of a lawyer to defend or advocate for their client, so answer A is correct.

34. In order to break up the _____ of the campaign trail, the candidate's wife picked up a _____ at the library to keep her entertained.

   A) Monotony, talisman
   B) Torpidity, laceration
   C) Exhilaration, magazine
   D) Vivacity, novel
   E) Tedium, tome

The correct answer is E:) Tedium, tome. Looking at the first answer blank, the wife would not need something to keep her entertained if the campaign trail were exhilarating or vivacious. So answers C and D can be eliminated. Considering the second answer blank, she would not go to the library to get either a talisman or a laceration. Therefore, answer E is the correct choice.

35. In order to ensure that he could not be a(n) _____ and be unfairly blamed if the advertising strategy failed, the marketing supervisor made a video of the meeting so that no one could later _____ their support of the plan.

   A) Scapegoat, rescind
   B) Effigy, repudiate
   C) Pariah, bolster
   D) Victim, proclaim
   E) Marshal, renounce

The correct answer is A:) Scapegoat, rescind. A person who is unfairly blamed for the mistakes of another is a scapegoat. Answer A also fits the second blank as well because the video would prevent people from changing, or rescinding, their support later. Therefore, answer A is the correct option.

36. The candidate was _____ that if he did not cooperate with the committee, they would remove their support for him and _____ against him instead.

   A) Anxious, gambol
   B) Tentative, conspire
   C) Apprehensive, collude
   D) Flippant, Amass
   E) Hesitant, vacillate

The correct answer is C:) Apprehensive, collude. You can assume that the candidate does not want to lose the support of the committee. This means that the only options that make sense in the first blank are options A, C and E. Of these three, only answer C makes sense for the second blank. Therefore, answer C is the correct option.

37. Despite years of ballet lessons, Samantha was still quite(a) _____, and when she tripped with the perfume bottle its _____ smell spread throughout the room.

   A) Clumsy, subtle
   B) Balletic, florid
   C) Graceful, lavish
   D) Lummox, potent
   E) Nimble, reprehensible

The correct answer is D:) Lummox, potent. Samantha would not have tripped if she were balletic, graceful, or nimble, so answer choices B, C, and E can all be eliminated. Answer A can be eliminated because the smell would not spread throughout the room as well if it were subtle as if it were potent. Therefore answer D is the correct option.

38. The grocery store manager found it absolutely _____ that the new employee actually believed that the beautiful, _____ rugs should be placed next to the fish section.

    A) Logical, opulent
    B) Sensible, lavish
    C) Absurd, austere
    D) Ludicrous, ornate
    E) Irrational, somber

The correct answer is D:) Ludicrous, ornate. Looking at the second answer blank, it would not make sense for the manager to consider the rugs both beautiful and either austere or somber, so answers C and E can be eliminated. Moving to the first answer blank, it is also unlikely that the manager would agree with putting fancy rugs by the smelly fish, eliminating options A and B. This means the correct answer must be D.

39. Wanting to _____ his role in the failed marketing strategy, the new intern tried to _____ his contribution.

    A) Mitigate, obscure
    B) Diminish, obviate
    C) Renown, burnish
    D) Exalt, underplay
    E) Elevate, underscore

The correct answer is A:) Mitigate, obscure. Because the strategy failed, the intern would want his role to be as little as possible so that he wasn't blamed. This means that answers A and B are the most likely options. It would not make sense to obviate his role if the intern wanted it to be ignored. Therefore, the correct answer is A.

40. The new office manager was strict and _____. It was a difficult transition for many of the employees who were accustomed to the easygoing and _____ manner of the old manager.

    A) Cantankerous, critical
    B) Demanding, jaded
    C) Fastidious, lax
    D) Oblivious, boorish
    E) Puerile, hypocritical

The correct answer is C:) Fastidious, lax. First considering the first word blank, it would not make sense to describe the new manager as both strict and oblivious or puerile. This means that options D and E can be eliminated. Considering the second blank, it would not make sense to describe the old manager as easygoing and jaded or critical. This means that answers A and B can be eliminated. Therefore, the correct answer is C.

41. As the two boxers began to circle each other, the talking came to a _____; because of the silence, the tension in the room was nearly _____.

    A) Hiatus, palpable
    B) Reprieve, paradoxical
    C) Climax, raucous
    D) Lull, covert
    E) Peak, tangible

The correct answer is A:) Hiatus, palpable. Because the room becomes silent, answers C and E can be eliminated because they do not fit for the first answer blank. If the room has silenced and the spectators are all watching the fight, it would not be described as paradoxical or covert. Therefore, the correct answer must be A. This indicates that the talking paused and the tension became extremely intense and tangible.

42. Although the meeting was called in order to discuss budget cutting strategies, the committee spent most of their time on _____ issues, such as the colors that should be used in the new logo and which marketing strategy had been successful in the past quarter.

    A) Central
    B) Cerebral
    C) Antiquated
    D) Paramount
    E) Peripheral

The correct answer is E:) Peripheral. The colors of the new logo and past strategies are not centrally important in budget cutting. Therefore, the word which makes the most sense in the blank is peripheral. Therefore, the correct answer is E.

43. The man was an expert on _____. He loved any animal that had a pouch, including kangaroos and koala bears.

    A) Mammals
    B) Marsupials
    C) Reptiles
    D) Invertebrates
    E) Olfactories

The correct answer is B:) Marsupials. Mammals, reptiles, and invertebrates do not have pouches. The term for animals with pouches is marsupials. Therefore, the correct answer is option B.

44. The class of first graders was quite _____, and the substitute had a difficult time _____ them to calm down after recess.

    A) Stupefying, goading
    B) Serene, requesting
    C) Raucous, cajoling
    D) Wary, belaboring
    E) Energetic, perusing

The correct answer is C:) Raucous, cajoling. Looking at the second blank, it is unlikely that the substitute would attempt to goad, belabor, or peruse the class into calming down. This eliminates answer choices A, D, and E. Of the remaining options, B and C, only C makes sense in the first answer blank. The teacher would not need to calm them down if they were being serene, but the substitute would need to calm them down for being raucous. Therefore, the correct answer is C.

45. In order to _____ the upset contractor, the painter agreed to _____ with the original pattern and paint the walls a sickly yellow as requested.

    A) Rancor, conform
    B) Appease, comply
    C) Placate, deviate
    D) Spite, ossify
    E) Pacify, diverge

The correct answer is B:) Appease, comply. If the painter is going along with the contractor's request, the only options that make sense for the second answer blank are comply and conform (options A and B). Also if the painter is trying to make the contractor happy, he is not trying to rancor or spite him. Therefore, the only option with satisfies both blanks is answer B.

46. When the investigator read the _____ to the document, they discovered that the company had stated that they would not _____ the natural resources by overfishing.

    A) Preamble, deplete
    B) Conclusion, replenish
    C) Introduction, belie
    D) Cacophony, diminish
    E) Obdurate, hamper

The correct answer is A:) Preamble, deplete. Answers D and E can be eliminated because they do not make sense as answers to the first blank. Documents do not have "obdurates" or "cacophonies." This leaves answers A, B, and C as possibilities. Overfishing would result in a lowering of fish populations, which is describe only by answer A, deplete. Therefore, the correct answer is A.

47. Jane was surprised by her brother's hypocrisy when she found a _____ in his words and actions.

    A) Vehemence
    B) Accord
    C) Discrepancy
    D) Concurrence
    E) Consensus

The correct answer is C:) Discrepancy. Hypocrisy is when a person's actions and their words are not in line with one another, or go against one another. The only word that describes this is discrepancy. Therefore, the correct answer is C.

48. The editor cautioned the authors not to use clichéd statements because they are _____ and common.

    A) Original
    B) Trite
    C) Wary
    D) Indolent
    E) Innovative

The correct answer is B:) Trite. A clichéd statement is one which is overused, common, and boring. The only word which embodies this is trite. Therefore, the correct answer is B.

49. Although he thought it was _____, the supervisor was awed by the company's plans to construct an entirely new office: it would be a towering _____ that would take three years to complete.

    A) Judicious, paradox
    B) Restrained, structure
    C) Brilliant, cacophony
    D) Immoderate, edifice
    E) Extravagant, hierarchy

The correct answer is D:) Immoderate, edifice. Considering the second blank, the only options that make sense as descriptions of a new office building are structure and edifice. This means that either B or D must be correct answer. Answer B can be eliminated because it does not make sense to say "although he thought it was restrained;" however, it does make sense to say "although he thought it was immoderate." This implies that despite the fact that the supervisor thinks it is too extravagant, he finds it impressive. Therefore, the correct answer is D.

50. Although she struggled under the _____ and difficult load, Jane was firm and _____ in her resolve to get the boxes to the top of the stairs.

    A) Indifferent, potable
    B) Pernicious, atrophying
    C) Dilatory, adamant
    D) Cumbersome, withering
    E) Ponderous, tenacious

The correct answer is E:) Ponderous, tenacious. It does not make sense to describe the load as difficult and indifferent, pernicious, or dilatory. Therefore, based on the first blank, only D or E fits as the answer. Considering the second blank, it does not make sense that she would be both firm and withering; however, it does make sense to say that she is firm and tenacious. Therefore, the correct answer is E.

51. The lawyer established his client's _____ by showing the jury that he couldn't have opened the spider cage due to his severe _____.

   A) Perspicacity, lung cancer
   B) Reliability, arthritis
   C) Culpability, allergies
   D) Alibi, arachnophobia
   E) Liability, trepidation

The correct answer is D:) Alibi, arachnophobia. A lawyer would not wish to establish their own client culpability or liability; however, they would want to establish their reliability or alibi. This makes either B or A the most probable answer. While arthritis is a possible reason a client couldn't open a cage, the fact that spiders are mentioned makes arachnophobia the more logical option. Therefore, the correct answer is D.

52. Because of the raging storm outside everyone was only able to get a _____ sleep, and the next day they were all _____ as they started their work.

   A) Languid, voracious
   B) Restful, lethargic
   C) Fitful, languid
   D) Erratic, vivacious
   E) Irregular, vibrant

The correct answer is C:) Fitful, languid. If there were a raging storm it is unlikely that people will get a restful or languid sleep, therefore options A and B can be eliminated. Looking at the second answer blank, if the sleep was not restful, the people would not be vivacious or vibrant – they would be tired. Therefore, answers D and E can be eliminated and the correct answer must be C.

53. Although the old office manager was lax with funds, the new manager was _____ and insisted that all of the employees fill out request forms before using any supplies.

   A) Lenient
   B) Gracious
   C) Fitful
   D) Averse
   E) Parsimonious

The correct answer is E:) Parsimonious. The line implies that the new manager is strict in contrast to the old manager. This means that the most likely answer is E, parsimonious, because it means frugal or thrifty.

54. The child had a strong _____ to reading, and _____ his book report to the last minute.

    A) Attraction, obfuscated
    B) Abhorrence, demurred
    C) Allure, obsequious
    D) Fascination, prepared
    E) Aversion, procrastinated

The correct answer is E:) Aversion, procrastinated. If the book report was done "at the last minute" this means that it was procrastinated, as in answer E. Furthermore, this is in line with the fact that the child has an aversion to reading, meaning they do not like to read. The correct answer is E.

55. After the children had spent the day looking for buried treasure in the backyard, the lawn was _____ with small holes.

    A) Atrophied
    B) Riddled
    C) Derided
    D) Profaned
    E) Tempered

The correct answer is B:) Riddled. If the children have been digging holes all day, there will be numerous holes. This statement is made with the word riddled which means "full of."

56. Jonathan hoped to win the chess game by _____; however, after he lost his queen he was _____ to his impending loss.

    A) Stratagem, resigned
    B) Skepticism, atrophied
    C) Cheating, belabored
    D) Renunciation, waylaid
    E) Submission, submitted

The correct answer is A:) Stratagem, resigned. Chess is a game which involves strategy. Skepticism and renunciation are not logical ways to play a game. Submission also would suggest losing rather than a hope to win. This leaves only stratagem and cheating. It would not make sense to be belabored to his impending loss. This leaves only answer A, that he was resigned to his impending loss.

57. The teacher gathered all the students together and tried to determine who the _____ of the fight was; however, the students tried to avoid trouble by _____ the truth.

   A) Completer, obviating
   B) Initiated, admitting
   C) Chronicler, charting
   D) Instigator, obfuscating
   E) None of the above

The correct answer is D:) Instigator, obfuscating. Considering the second blank, the students could not avoid trouble by charting or admitting the truth. Similarly, obviating the truth would be the equivalent of admitting it. This leaves only option D, obfuscating. Obfuscating or hiding the truth, however, would be a way of possibly avoiding trouble for fighting. Therefore, the correct answer is D.

58. After falling from the tall _____, the speaker _____ to the ground.

   A) Edifice, clamored
   B) Orifice, commandeered
   C) Podium, plummeted
   D) Depression, elevated
   E) Mountain, jaded

The correct answer is C:) Podium, plummeted. Answers B and D can be eliminated because depressions and orifices are not tall. This leaves edifice, podium, and mountain. Although mountains are tall you cannot fall off of them, so answer E can be eliminated. Moving to the second blank, after falling it would not make sense to say that the speaker clamored to the ground, but it would make sense to way he plummeted. Therefore, the correct answer is C.

59. After he had some time _____ on the matter, the old man decided to _____ his statement because he could not really remember what had happened.

    A) Pondering, reinforce
    B) Meditating, emphasize
    C) Tempering, withdraw
    D) Placating, extend
    E) Ruminate, retract

The correct answer is E:) Ruminate, retract. If the old man is not sure he remembers what happened, he would not extend, emphasize, or reinforce his statement. This means that options A, B, and D can be eliminated. It does not make sense to place the word tempering in the first blank, so option C can be eliminated. Therefore, the correct answer is E.

60. The baker _____ her chocolate so that it would drizzle nicely over the strawberries.

    A) Elevated
    B) Obfuscated
    C) Tempered
    D) Decremented
    E) Egressed

The correct answer is C:) Tempered. For chocolate to drizzle it needs to be softened because it is solid at room temperature. This is the meaning of the word tempered, therefore it is the correct option.

61. The old lady had many _____ that he she had collected during her life, and her husband was _____ of her insistence on keeping them all because they made her house appear cluttered.

    A) Drones, critical
    B) Trinkets, censorious
    C) Enigmas, understanding
    D) Charms, supportive
    E) None of the above

The correct answer is B:) Trinkets, censorious. Looking at the first blank, it is not possible to collect either drones or enigmas, so options A and C can be eliminated. Considering the second blank, the husband would not be supportive of her collection if he felt it made the house cluttered. Therefore, the correct answer B.

62. When the manager announced the coming pay cuts, the employees all _____ to state their objection before the decision was _____ by the board of direc-tors.

    A) Clamored, ratified
    B) Rushed, equivocated
    C) Epitomized, erred
    D) Languid, eradicated
    E) Labored, vetoed

The correct answer is A:) Clamored, ratified. Answered C and D can be eliminated because the words epitomized and languid do not fit the context of the first blank. However, the employees would clamor, be rushed, or labored to object to pay cuts. The employees would have no need to object if the board of directors was vetoing the decision, and it would not make sense to insert equivocated in the second answer blank. This leaves only answer A as the correct option.

63. When the man refused to testify in the _____ case the police issued him a _____ so that he had to testify that the man was in fact the burglar.

    A) Robbery, parody
    B) Arson, conflagration
    C) Murder, summons
    D) Brief, excusal
    E) Larceny, subpoena

The correct answer is E:) Larceny, subpoena. Because the man is being called to testify in a burglary case, answers B (arson), C (murder), and D (brief) can be eliminated as possibilities. A subpoena forces a person to testify, so answer E is the correct answer.

64. The scientist argued that cockroaches are essentially _____, and are the only creatures that would survive a nuclear war.

    A) Pallid
    B) Ostentatious
    C) Indelible
    D) Defoliate
    E) Serendipitous

The correct answer is C:) Indelible. The word indelible means incapable of being wiped out. This is what is described by the fact that they would survive a nuclear war. There-fore, the correct answer is C.

65. Jared had long been afraid of heights and was _____ standing at the top of the Eiffel Tower, and was much more _____ upon reaching the ground again.

    A) Timorous, nervous
    B) Placid, vociferous
    C) Staunch, timorous
    D) Petrified, placid
    E) Tranquil, serene

The correct answer is D:) Petrified, placid. If he is afraid of heights he would be afraid at the top of a tall building, leaving answers A and D as possibilities. Upon returning to the ground he would be relaxed, not nervous, and answer A can be eliminated. Therefore, the correct answer is D.

66. Those in attendance at the funeral were all quite _____, though his death came as no surprise. He had been suffering from _____ heart failure.

    A) Vivacious, hereditary
    B) Melancholy, congenital
    C) Regretful, subtle
    D) Glum, unexpected
    E) None of the above

The correct answer is B:) Melancholy, congenital. The people would not be vivacious at a funeral, so option A can be eliminated. Because his death was not a surprise, subtle and unexpected can be eliminated as options. This leaves only option B as the correct answer. This is logical because the guests would be melancholy, or sad, at the funeral. Furthermore, congenital heart failure (a problem which is present from birth) would not come as a surprise either.

67. Sally knew that she was no _____ when after she had mixed all of the chemicals together they coalesced into a brown _____ blob.

    A) Alchemist, amorphous
    B) Chemist, stratified
    C) Historian, stolid
    D) Author, nebulous
    E) Somnambulist, shapeless

The correct answer is A:) Alchemist, amorphous. Considering the first answer blank, answers C, D, and E can be eliminated because none of these individuals would be mixing chemicals. A blob would not be described as stratified so answer B can be eliminated. This leaves option A, that the blob was shapeless which is the correct answer.

68. The judge ruled that the evidence could not be admitted in court because it was _____, and it was unfair for the _____ to wait until so late in the trial to share it.

    A) Amorphous, defense
    B) Dubious, dunce
    C) Apocryphal, plaintiff
    D) Stupefying, lampoon
    E) Substantial, witness

The correct answer is C:) Apocryphal, plaintiff. Considering the second answer blank, options B, D, and E can be eliminated because dunces, lampoons, and witnesses do not present evidence in trial. The judge would not refuse to admit evidence because it was amorphous, but the judge would refuse to admit evidence if it had doubtful origin (i.e., if it were apocryphal). Therefore, the correct answer is option C.

69. After _____ her work to stay out all night with friends, Jen felt that she had no choice but to _____ the paper that was due in her English class by finding one on the internet.

    A) Commencing, obscure
    B) Procrastinating, plagiarize
    C) Initiating, irritate
    D) Postponing, complete
    E) Nullifying, obviate

The correct answer is B:) Procrastinating, plagiarize. The first part of the sentence indicates that Jen stayed out with friends instead of writing her paper. This means that answers A (commencing) and C (initiating) can be eliminated because she did not start her work. It also would not make sense to say that she nullified her work so answer E can be eliminated. Looking at the second blank, if she copies a paper off of this internet this would be plagiarizing. This means that the correct answer is B.

70. The suspect agreed to _____ her Miranda rights because she didn't want to make the officers suspicious.

    A) Hold
    B) Support
    C) Waive
    D) Validate
    E) Officiate

The correct answer is C:) Waive. The Miranda rights have to do with the rights a person has when they are being investigated. If the suspect doesn't want to make the officers suspicious she would not hold, support, or validate them because she would want to cooperate. It also doesn't make sense to say that she officiated her Miranda rights. However, it does make sense that she would waive, or give up, her rights to avoid suspicion. Therefore, the correct answer is C, waive.

71. The manager decided not to hire the applicant because of her _____ manner: she came _____ into the interview and giggled at most of the questions.

    A) Oblivious, stolidly
    B) Ebullient, punctually
    C) Obscure, tardy
    D) Vacuous, tittering
    E) Obtuse, eccentrically

The correct answer is D:) Vacuous, tittering. Any of the options could possibly fit into the first blank, so for this question it is necessary to consider the second blank first. Punctuality is not a reason to dislike someone, so answer B can be eliminated. If the applicant were obtuse she would not enter the room eccentrically so answer E can be eliminated. The applicant would not giggle through the interview if she were stolid so answer A can be eliminated. She would giggle through the interview if she were vacuous and tittering, however. Therefore, the correct answer is option D.

72. The comedian was _____, and the crowd could not stop laughing at his jokes despite his _____ and unique sense of humor.

    A) Uproarious, unorthodox
    B) Enfranchised, ignominy
    C) Immoderate, lackluster
    D) Lavish, tedious
    E) Raucous, hypocritical

The correct answer is A:) Uproarious, unorthodox. If the comedian is funny this means that the options that fit into the first answer blank are option A, uproarious, and answer E, raucous. It would not be logical to say that he had a hypocritical sense of humor, so answer E can be eliminated. It does make sense to call a sense of humor both unique and unorthodox. Therefore, the correct answer is A.

73. The psychologist insisted to her client that his love of and _____ with mythical creatures was unhealthy, and she brought in many experts to _____ the existence of vampires.

    A) Fanaticism, emphasize
    B) Obsession, debunk
    C) Trepidation, immoderate
    D) Fixation, accentuate
    E) Phobia, renounce

The correct answer is B:) Obsession, debunk. Considering the first answer blank, the client would not have both love and fear of mythical creatures, so options C and E can be eliminated. Moving to the second answer blank, the psychologist would not want to accentuate or emphasize this fear, so options A and D can be eliminated. This leaves option B as the correct answer.

74. The professor gave a very helpful _____ of the political climate leading up to World War I, and the students were all impressed with his _____ knowledge of the subject.

    A) Inclination, insincere
    B) Exegesis, trivial
    C) Magnate, maladroit
    D) Lecture, lithe
    E) Delineation, vast

The correct answer is E:) Delineation, vast. Both answer A and C do not fit the context of the first sentence, so these options can be eliminated. Lecture, exegesis, and delineation, however, could all describe the professor teaching, and they make sense as options. Considering the second answer blank, if the lecture is helpful the students would not then consider the professor's knowledge trivial or lithe. This means that the correct answer is E. The students believe the teacher to have a great knowledge of the subject.

75. The criminal avoided _____ by the government by fleeing to a country that would not allow _____.

    A) Chastisement, extradition
    B) Reward, deportation
    C) Praise, expulsion
    D) Laud, longevity
    E) Rebuke, immigrants

The correct answer is A:) Chastisement, extradition. Considering the first answer blank, options B, C, and D can be eliminated because a criminal would not be avoiding reward or praise from the government. Answer E can further be eliminated because the criminal could not flee to a country that does not allow immigrants, but he would be benefitted by fleeing to a country that would not extradite him (or send him back to the United States). This means that the correct answer is A.

76. Lawrence loved his job as a detective because he could bring _____ individuals to justice; however, he disliked always being the _____ of bad news and telling people that their loved ones had been murdered.

    A) Lethargic, instigator
    B) Impious, harbinger
    C) Loquacious, perfidy
    D) Nefarious, lummox
    E) Disreputable, obfuscator

The correct answer is B:) Impious, harbinger. Considering the first answer blank, answers A and C can be eliminated because detectives bring evil people to justice, not lethargic (tired) or loquacious (talkative) people. Answer D can be eliminated because lummox describes a clumsy person, and does not fit in second blank. Answer E can be eliminated because detectives do not obscure or obfuscate information. This means that the correct answer must be option B.

77. Because of the incoming storm, the pilot _____ in his decision to go flying and parked his plane in the _____.

    A) Continued, runway
    B) Wavered, garage
    C) Waned, epistolary
    D) Faltered, hangar
    E) Clamored, shed

The correct answer is D:) Faltered, hangar. The sentence indicates that the pilot chose not to fly, this means that options A and E can be eliminated because they both indicate that the pilot chose to fly anyway. The correct answer must be answer D because a hangar is in fact where planes are parked, and the word faltered does describe the fact that he changed his mind.

78. Due to the captain's excellent work directing the crew, the ship was able to emerge from the _____ that it had been caught in _____ and in working condition.

    A) Turbulence, destroyed
    B) Maelstrom, unscathed
    C) Celerity, Intact
    D) Vortex, demolished
    E) Tranquility, choleric

The correct answer is B:) Maelstrom, unscathed. The crew would not need directing if the sea were calm, so answer E can be eliminated. It also does not make sense to say that the ship had been caught in celerity, so option C can be eliminated. The sentence further indicates that the ship emerged in working condition, so answers A and D can be eliminated because the ship was not destroyed or demolished in the storm. Therefore, the correct answer must be B: the ship was caught in a violent storm (maelstrom), but emerged unharmed (unscathed).

79. After the _____ in which the political candidates met, they began fierce campaigns in which they attempted to _____ each other and dissuade voters.

    A) Debate, chary
    B) Chronicle, malign
    C) Caucus, vilify
    D) Convention, advocate
    E) Conference, sponsor

The correct answer is C:) Caucus, vilify. Political candidates would meet in a debate, caucus, convention, or conference, but not in a chronicle, so option B can be eliminated. Options D and E can be eliminated because opposing candidates would not try to help each other's campaigns by sponsoring or advocating them. Answer A can be eliminated because candidates also would not chary each other. Therefore, the correct answer is C, that the candidates worked to blacken each other's names (which is indicated by the word vilify).

80. Amber was frustrated because after a month of working she still had not received
_____, and could not afford to pay her rent.

    A) Vilification
    B) Petulance
    C) Remuneration
    D) Apathy
    E) Renown

The correct answer is C:) Remuneration. Vilification, petulance, apathy, and renown
may fit in the blank, but none of them would allow Amber to pay her rent. However,
remuneration or payment for work would allow her to pay her rent. Therefore answer
C is the most logical option.

81. The guilty criminal hoped to _____ the police with his _____
claims of innocence, and refusal to admit to the crime.

    A) Censure, covert
    B) Solicit, obstinate
    C) Confuse, idle
    D) Exasperate, chary
    E) Beguile, tenacious

The correct answer is E:) Beguile, tenacious. A criminal would not wish to censure or
solicit the police, especially if he was guilty. Therefore, options A and B can be eliminated because they do not fit the first answer blank. Answers C and D can be eliminated
because the criminal would not make idle or chary claims. Therefore, the correct answer is option E.

82. The mediator hoped to _____ the two arguing parties; however, their
_____ resulted in a continuation of the argument that lasted for many
years.

    A) Reconcile, altruism
    B) Conciliate, intransigence
    C) Exasperate, antagonism
    D) Underscore, vehemence
    E) Stupefy, bigotry

The correct answer is B:) Conciliate, intransigence. A mediator would not want to ex-
asperate, underscore, or stupefy two arguing parties. It is the mediator's job to bring
arguments to an end by reconciling or conciliating the parties. The argument would not
perpetuate if the parties were altruistic, so answer A can be eliminated. Therefore, the
correct answer is option B.

83. The doctor proscribed a _____ to help ease the pain of the man's injury; however, he warned him that it was merely a _____ and would not cure him, but would make it more bearable.

    A) Analgesic, anthology
    B) Sedative, panacea
    C) Respite, enigma
    D) Restorative, palliative
    E) None of the above

The correct answer is D:) Restorative, palliative. Looking at the first answer blank, an analgesic, sedative, or restorative would all help ease the man's pain. A palliative is a substance that improves something but does not cure it. Therefore, palliative is the most logical word choice. Therefore, the correct answer is D.

84. The supervisor was upset by the Erika's _____ disregard of the rules: company policy stated that employees need to treat all clients respectfully, and she had knowingly insulted the elderly man by calling him a _____.

    A) Flagrant, dotard
    B) Blatant, patron
    C) Unintentional, bombast
    D) Inadvertent, sage
    E) Careless, misogynist

The correct answer is A:) Flagrant, dotard. Considering the first blank, if Erika knowingly insulted the client, her insult could not have been inadvertent, careless, or unintentional. This leaves only options A and B. It would not be insulting if Erika had called the man a patron, therefore the correct option is answer A.

85. The manager informed the receptionist that he could not _____ her treatment of clients, and that she would be fired if she continued giving _____ looks to everyone who waked through the door.

    A) Tolerate, obsequious
    B) Condone, glacial
    C) Accept, compassionate
    D) Disregard, amiable
    E) Criticize, puerile

The correct answer is B:) Condone, glacial. The manager is threatening to fire the receptionist, so he isn't happy with her behavior. This means that options C and E can be eliminated. Considering the second answer blank, the manager would not have a problem with her giving obsequious or amiable looks. Therefore, the correct answer is option B.

86. The millionaire insisted that the only way to _____ a great fortune was to save as much money as you could each month from the time you were very young.

    A) Lose
    B) Deter
    C) Envenom
    D) Waylay
    E) Amass

The correct answer is E:) Amass. Saving money would be a way to build a fortune, so the correct answer is E.

87. The lawyers hoped that a _____ could be reached so that they could end the long and seemingly _____ process of their clients' divorce.

    A) Accord, brief
    B) Reconciliation, ephemeral
    C) Dispute, eternal
    D) Quarrel, endless
    E) Consensus, interminable

The correct answer is E:) Consensus, interminable. If they want to end the case, the lawyers would not be hoping for a quarrel or a dispute. Therefore, options C and D can be eliminated. The process would not be described as both long and brief or ephemeral so options A and B can be eliminated. Therefore, the correct answer is E.

88. The judge decided to stop the trial for a short _____ so that the jury members could go to the bathroom and get something to drink because they were _____.

    A) Respite, parched
    B) Perfidy, dubious
    C) Interval, satiated
    D) Profanity, languid
    E) Recess, assuaged

The correct answer is A:) Respite, parched. A trial would not be stopped for a perfidy or profanity so answers B and D can be eliminated since they do not fit the first answer blank. The jury would not need water if they were satiated (answer C) or assuaged (answer E) so these can both be eliminated as well. Therefore, the correct answer is option A.

89. The funeral guests all attempted to give _____ to the grieving widow: they told her to remember the good times, and not to _____ to her feelings of anguish.

    A) Comfort, resist
    B) Irritation, succumb
    C) Solace, submit
    D) Ire, acquiesce
    E) None of the above

The correct answer is C:) Solace, submit. A funeral guest would not want to make a grieving widow irritated or angry, so options B and D can be eliminated. Rather, they would give her solace and comfort. However, answer A can be eliminated because they would wish for her to resist feelings of anguish, not submit to them. Therefore, the correct answer is option C.

90. The man was _____ and bluntly honest in his statement that he found his neighbor's cooking to be _____ and inedible.

    A) Frank, palatable
    B) Candid, odious
    C) Covert, abhorrent
    D) Blunt, potable
    E) Subversive, repulsive

The correct answer is B:) Candid, odious. Considering the first blank, if the man is bluntly honest he must be either frank or candid, so all of the options except for A and B can be eliminated. It would be illogical to describe food as both palatable and inedible so option A can be eliminated. This leaves only option B as the correct answer.

91. The judge decided that he could not officiate in the case because he could not be _____ since the defendant was his neighbor and he considered him to be a _____ and untrustworthy person.

   A) Impartial, disreputable
   B) Neutral, honorable
   C) Biased, upstanding
   D) Bigoted, degenerate
   E) Bereaved, nefarious

The correct answer is A:) Impartial, disreputable. The judge would not refuse to officiate in a case based on feelings of bereavement so option E can be eliminated since it does not fit the first blank. Options C and D can be eliminated because it would not make sense for the judge to try to be bigoted or biased as that would be unethical. Option B can be eliminated because it would be illogical to describe the man as both untrustworthy and honorable. Therefore the correct answer is option A.

92. The tour guide taught the people that the name Koala Bear is actually a _____ because koalas are not bears at all, they are marsupials.

   A) Dilettante
   B) Prerogative
   C) Identifier
   D) Misnomer
   E) Candor

The correct answer is D:) Misnomer. The tour guide is describing the fact that the Koala Bears name is misleading or poorly chosen. This is the meaning of the word misnomer. Therefore, the correct answer is option D.

93. The new manager showed that he was a much more _____ worker than his _____ (the old manager) by taking half as many breaks during the day.

   A) Diligent, predecessor
   B) Perfunctory, ancestor
   C) Pretentious, supervisor
   D) Conscientious, replacement
   E) Obligatory, descendant

The correct answer is A:) Diligent, predecessor. Looking at the second answer blank, the previous manager would be referred to as the new manager's predecessor, and not his ancestor, supervisor, replacement, or descendant. Therefore answer A must be the correct option.

94. In order to _____ the flow of water downstream, and instead keep it near the city, the townspeople built a _____.

    A) Bolster, gaunt
    B) Hinder, dike
    C) Encourage, barrier
    D) Hamper, fortification
    E) Encumber, bulwark

The correct answer is B:) Hinder, dike. If they wanted to keep the water near the city then they townspeople would not bolster or encourage its flow, so options A and C can be eliminated. Furthermore, a dam or dike is what is built to stop the flow of river water. Therefore, the correct answer is option B.

95. Although the woman initially felt that the man's gifts were _____ and generous, when he gave her the tenth pair of diamond earrings she began to feel that it was _____.

    A) Magnanimous, gaunt
    B) Meager, superfluous
    C) Obtuse, irksome
    D) Pretentious, perfunctory
    E) Munificent, gratuitous

The correct answer is E:) Munificent, gratuitous. If the man's gifts are generous, then the woman would not consider them to be meager. Furthermore, she did not initially object to them or consider them obtuse or pretentious as both have negative and rude connotations. This leaves options A and E as possible answers. Based on the second part of the sentence the gifts are excessive without cause which is the meaning of the word gratuitous. Therefore, the correct answer is E.

96. The mother made many _____ trips to the store to buy her son's birthday gifts without him knowing.

    A) Clandestine
    B) Overt
    C) Candid
    D) Inexorable
    E) Unwitting

The correct answer is A:) Clandestine. If the mother does not want her son to know about her trips to the store than she would be covert and secretive. This is the meaning of the word clandestine. Therefore the correct answer is A.

97. The Swedish girl felt quite _____ because of her light and _____ skin tone in comparison to the African children around her when she went on a service trip to Nigeria.

    A) Inconspicuous, pale
    B) Ostentatious, pallid
    C) Flamboyant, perfunctory
    D) Counterfeit, deliberate
    E) Discreet, resplendent

The correct answer is B:) Ostentatious, pallid. A native Swede would have very light skin, whereas the native African children would have very dark skin. This means that she would stand out, so the options inconspicuous (A), counterfeit (D), and discreet (E) can be eliminated. Furthermore, it would not make sense to describe her skin tone as perfunctory, so option C can be eliminated. This means that option B is the correct answer.

98. The teacher worked quickly to _____ the insulting and rude statements from the white board, and to _____ the children for their insensitive and unacceptable behavior.

    A) Subterfuge, chastise
    B) Emphasize, rebuke
    C) Efface, censure
    D) Obliterate, congratulate
    E) Eradicate, laud

The correct answer is C:) Efface, censure. Because the statements are rude and insulting, the teacher would wish to remove them from the board. This means that options A and B can be eliminated because they do not convey this. Considering the second answer blank, the teacher would rebuke the children for being rude, so options D and E can be eliminated because they convey praise. This means that the correct answer is C.

99. The downfall of the witness was his _____ temper. The lawyer did not want to put him on the stand because he could not predict how he would react under cross-examination when the defense tried to make him look _____ and foolish.

    A) Meticulous, illogical
    B) Tangible, nonsensical
    C) Noxious, lithe
    D) Volatile, irrational
    E) Obstreperous, sagacious

The correct answer is D:) Volatile, irrational. Options A and B can be eliminated because they do not fit the first answer blank: it is illogical to describe a temper as either meticulous or tangible. Options C and E can be eliminated because they do not fit the second answer blank: it would not make sense to describe the man as both foolish and lithe or sagacious. Therefore, the correct answer is D.

100. In an attempt to _____ the students' confidence, and make them feel good about their work, the teacher decided to _____ with their request for an early recess.

    A) Reinforce, refuse
    B) Traverse, conform
    C) Subvert, acquiesce
    D) Bolster, comply
    E) Augment, balk

The correct answer is D:) Bolster, comply. If the teacher is trying to make the students feel good about their work, then the word in the first answer blank must convey an increase in confidence. This means that only answers A, D, or E can be correct, and answers B and C can be eliminated. If the teacher wants to reward the students then the word in the second answer blank must convey that she agreed with their request, so options A and E can be eliminated. Therefore, the correct answer is D.

Sentence Completion Sample Test Question Answer Key

1. E	37. D	73. B
2. B	38. D	74. E
3. A	39. A	75. A
4. C	40. C	76. B
5. B	41. A	77. D
6. E	42. E	78. B
7. D	43. B	79. C
8. D	44. C	80. C
9. B	45. A	81. E
10. A	46. A	82. B
11. C	47. C	83. D
12. A	48. B	84. A
13. E	49. D	85. B
14. A	50. E	86. E
15. D	51. D	87. E
16. C	52. C	88. A
17. E	53. E	89. C
18. B	54. E	90. B
19. D	55. B	91. A
20. D	56. A	92. D
21. A	57. D	93. A
22. C	58. D	94. B
23. E	59. E	95. E
24. B	60. C	96. A
25. D	61. B	97. B
26. D	62. A	98. C
27. C	63. E	99. D
28. A	64. C	100. D
29. E	65. D	
30. B	66. B	
31. C	67. A	
32. D	68. C	
33. A	69. B	
34. E	70. C	
35. A	71. D	
36. C	72. A	

Passage-Based Reading

This section will give you a chance to practice reading a passage and answering the test question, just like on the real test. Take your time to read carefully so you will get the full meaning of the text and the test question. Make sure to read through the test question rationale in order to learn how to better understand any passage you have to read. Not only will you be able to correctly eliminate answer choices, you can understand the reasoning of why one answer is more correct than another. The best and really only way to increase your ability of reading and analyzing passages is to practice. Carefully study and review this section.

PASSAGE

(1) Another thing that surprised me was the quantity of silver that was in circulation. (2) I certainly never saw so much silver at one time in my life, as during the week that we were at Monterey. (3) The truth is, they have no credit system, no banks, and no way of investing money but in cattle. (4) They have no circulating medium but silver and hides–which the sailors call "California bank notes." (5) Everything that they buy they must pay for in one or the other of these things.

Two Years Before the Mast
By Richard Henry Dana
Chapter 13: Trading- A British Sailor

1. The word "credit" in line 3 most closely means

    A) Honor
    B) Trustworthiness
    C) Source of pride
    D) Acknowledgement
    E) Payment based on future availability of cash

All of the answers provide a possible synonym of the word credit; however, only one of the possibilities fits the specific context of the passage. The passage is discussing the monetary system of the people in Monterey. Furthermore, the specific line also mentions banks and investments. This makes the most likely answer E.

2. The word "things" at the end of line 5 refers to

    A) "Banks" (line 3)
    B) "Everything that they buy" (line 5)
    C) "Silver and hides" (line 4)
    D) "California bank notes" (line 4)
    E) None of the above

The word "things" is used to refer to payment methods. Although California bank notes (option D) is one of the items that the word things refers to, only answer C correctly identifies both objects which the word things is used to refer to. Therefore, the correct answer is C.

3. The speaker in the passage most likely considers the trading system he describes to be

    A) Exemplary
    B) Inferior
    C) Commendable
    D) Diffident
    E) Monotonous

The options of exemplary and commendable would both indicate that the speaker is impressed by the system. However, in the first line he states that he is surprised by all of the silver trade. The tone of the passage also clearly conveys that the speaker is unsure about the system, and finds it inefficient. Therefore, the correct answer is inferior, option B.

PASSAGE

(1) And the worst of it was, and the root of it all, ... that consequently one was not only unable to change but could do absolutely nothing. (2) Thus it would follow, as the result of acute consciousness, that one is not to blame in being a scoundrel; ... (3) But enough. ... Ech, I have talked a lot of nonsense, but what have I explained? (4) How is enjoyment in this to be explained? (5) But I will explain it. (6) I will get to the bottom of it! (7) That is why I have taken up my pen. ...

Notes from the Underground
By Fyodor Dostoyevsky
Part 1: Chapter II

4. The speaker in the passage can best be described as

  A) Insincere
  B) Caustic
  C) Unstable
  D) Stolid
  E) Unemotional

Answer A can be eliminated because while the speaker does not follow a particularly logical train of thought, he does seem adamant in attempting to make some conclusion. Answer B can be eliminated because the speaker, while illogical, is not bitter or hurtful in his comments. Answer D can be eliminated because the speaker is clearly passionate. He proclaims "I will get to the bottom of it!" in line 6, and is not dull or unemotional. Therefore, the correct answer is C, unstable. The speaker in the passage seems to be rambling through what he is saying, and even admits to have explained "nothing," and to be getting enjoyment out of it.

5. As used in line 2, what is the meaning of the word acute?

  A) Sensitive
  B) Crucial
  C) Keen, sharp
  D) Small
  E) Dull

Answers B and D can be eliminated because it does not make sense to describe consciousness either crucial or small. Answer A can be eliminated because it does not fit into the context. The speaker refers to the ability to change one's status in life, and about the ability to explain enjoyment. Answer E can be eliminated because it is actually an antonym of the word acute. Therefore, the correct answer is C.

PASSAGE

(1) In 1844 Charles Dickens wrote to Forster: (2) "Chigwell, my dear fellow, is the greatest place in the world. (3) Name your day for going. (4) Such a delicious old inn facing the church–such a lovely ride–such forest scenery–such an out-of-the-way rural place–such a sexton! (5) I say again, Name your day." (6) This is surely sufficient recommendation for any place.

What to See in England
By Gordon Home
Chigwell, Essex

6. How does the author of this passage think of Charles Dickens?

   A) Respectfully
   B) Distastefully
   C) Indifferently
   D) Uncertainly
   E) Diminutively

The passage concludes by reinforcing the statement made by Charles Dickens. The author indicates that if Dickens recommended it, then Chigwell must be a nice place. Clearly the author has high respect for Charles Dickens. This eliminates all of the options except for A.

7. The passage was most likely written when?

   A) Before 1844
   B) Early in 1844
   C) Late in 1784
   D) After 1844
   E) Cannot be determined

Because the passage consists of a quote that was written in 1844 it must have been written after that. Therefore, the correct answer is option D.

8. Based on the passage, the author wishes to

    A) Stop people from visiting Chigwell
    B) Determine someone's plans for the next day
    C) Get someone interested in studying nature
    D) Convince people to go to Chigwell
    E) None of the above

The author quotes a passage of Charles Dickens to serve as a glowing description of Chigwell. He would not do this if he wished to stop people from visiting the area; therefore, answer A can be eliminated. Answer B can be eliminated because at no point in the passage does the speaker ask any questions of a third party, or reference them in any way. Rather, it is directed to a general audience. Answer C can be eliminated because the passage is descriptive a specific place, not nature in general. This leaves answer D as the correct option. The author offers a glowing recommendation of Chigwell.

9. As used in line 4, the word delicious most closely means

    A) Pleasant to taste
    B) Delightful
    C) Palatable
    D) Well-maintained
    E) Grand

Although answers A and C are the most common meanings of the work delicious, it would be illogical for someone to describe a building in this way. Although it would make sense to describe a building as well-maintained or grand, neither of these words are a definition or synonym of the word delicious. Delightful is both a possible synonym of the word delicious, and makes sense in the context of the passage. Therefore, the correct answer is B.

10. The phrase "name your day" in line 5 indicates that Dickens

    A) Does not want to go to Chigwell ever again
    B) Will go if he is given sufficient notice and feels like it that day
    C) Is testing Forster to see if he was paying attention
    D) Wants to know what day it is
    E) Would be pleased to go any day

The passage as a whole involves Charles Dickens stating Chigwell as a nice place to visit. Because of this, options A, C, and D can all be eliminated since they are irrelevant. Based on the fact that he refers to Chigwell as one of the greatest places on earth, and is clearly impressed with it, it is more likely that he is indicating that he would be willing to go at any time. Therefore, the correct answer is E.

PASSAGE

First published as one of the Oxford Pamphlets, October 1914:

(1) To the English mind the German political doctrine is so incredibly stupid that for many long years, (2) while men in high authority in the German Empire, ministers, generals, and professors, expounded that doctrine at great length and with perfect clearness, (3) hardly anyone could be found in England to take it seriously, or to regard it as anything but the vapourings of a crazy sect. (4) England knows better now; the scream of the guns has awakened her.

England and the War
By Walter Raleigh
Might Is Right

11. The "scream of guns" referred to in line 4 is most likely referring to

   A) A fictional war
   B) The American Revolution
   C) Austro-Prussian War
   D) WWI
   E) WWII

The summary at the beginning of the passage indicates that it was published in 1914, just after the beginning of WWI. Because Germany and England were against one another in this war, this makes D, WWI, the most likely possibility.

12. The author of the passage is most likely

   A) German
   B) Irish
   C) English
   D) Portuguese
   E) Austrian

The passage describes the English sentiment about the German people and it describes the current English mentality. Also, the excerpt was published in the Oxford Pamphlets, an English political pamphlet. Therefore, it is most likely that the author of the passage was English.

13. As used in line 3, "vapourings" most closely means

   A) Boastings
   B) Contentions
   C) Visible exhalations
   D) A thick fog
   E) Advertisements

Of the options given, A, C, and D are all correct definitions of the word "vapourings." Because the passage is talking about the propaganda and political doctrines of the German people, boastings makes the most sense of these options. Also, people do not have "thick fogs." Therefore, the correct answer is A, boastings.

PASSAGE

The speaker of the passage has just read a plaque on a door indicating that Proctors and Rogues were not welcome, but all other poor travelers are.

(1) "Now," said I to myself, as I looked at the knocker, "I know I am not a Proctor; I wonder whether I am a Rogue!"

(2) Upon the whole, though Conscience reproduced two or three pretty faces which might have had smaller attraction for a moral Goliath[1] than they had had for me, who am but a Tom Thumb[2] in that way, I came to the conclusion that I was not a Rogue.

1. A giant referenced in the bible.
2. A fictional character smaller than his father's thumb.

The Seven Poor Travelers
By Charles Dickens
Chapter 1: In the Old City of Rochester

14. The speaker in the passage is

    A) Flippant
    B) Judgmental
    C) Didactic
    D) Open-minded
    E) Self-deprecating

Answer A can be eliminated because the speaker pauses to honestly consider whether he is a proctor or a rogue before he knocks, showing respect for other people in general. The speaker does not give the impression of being either judgmental or didactic because he states himself that he is a "Tom Thumb" in terms of morality, and that he has made some questionable decisions in his lifetime. The speaker can also not be described as self-deprecating because he seems to have no qualms with the fact that he has made mistakes, and still does not consider himself a rogue. He can, however, be described as open-minded for this reason, and because he is willing to consider the question honestly. Therefore, the correct answer is D.

15. The speaker in the passage considers himself to be

    A) A highly moral person, despite not being a Proctor
    B) A moderately moral person, because they are a judge
    C) Outside the realm of normal moral judgments
    D) Very immoral, to the point of being a rogue
    E) Not very moral, although not a rogue either

The speaker indicates that he is not a moral Goliath. The first footnote describes Goliath as a giant. Therefore, the speaker is saying that he is not a highly or strictly moral person. Further, the speaker indicates that he is somewhat a "Tom Thumb" when it comes to morality. The second footnote describes Tom Thumb as a tiny person. Therefore, the most logical answer is E.

16. As used in line 1, the word knocker refers to

    A) A person who knocks
    B) A person who finds fault with everything
    C) A decorative door ornament used for knocking
    D) Promptness
    E) Persistent critic

The summary prior to the passage indicates that the speaker is standing before a door. This makes it unlikely that the work knocker is referring to A, B, or E because each involves a specific person. The fact that he describes staring at the knocker means that "promptness" cannot be the correct answer because it is not a visible object. Therefore, the correct answer is C, a decorative door ornament used for knocking.

PASSAGE

(1) Had you called Austin Ford an amateur detective he would have been greatly annoyed. (2) He argued that his position was similar to that of the dramatic critic. (3) The dramatic critic warned the public against bad plays; Ford warned it against bad men. (4) Having done that, he left it to the public to determine whether the bad man should thrive or perish.

(5) When the managing editor told him of his appointment to London, Ford had protested that his work lay in New York; that of London and the English, except as a tourist and sight-seer, he knew nothing.

The Amateur
By Richard Harding Davis
Part I

17. Austin Ford's occupation is that of a

    A) Private Eye
    B) Journalist
    C) Amateur detective
    D) Theater critic
    E) Newscaster

The passage indicates that Ford would be annoyed at the description of "amateur detective," so this is an unlikely option. Furthermore, it indicates that he does not catch or follow criminals, merely informs the public about them. This means that answers A and C can both be eliminated. Ford believes himself to be similar to a theater critic, but this means that he is not one. Therefore, answer D can be eliminated. In line five it refers to a managing editor, which means that Ford's occupation most likely has to do with writing. Therefore, newscaster (answer E) can be eliminated. Therefore, the correct answer is B, journalist.

18. As used in line 1, the word amateur means

    A) Inexperienced
    B) Excellent
    C) Insubordinate
    D) Professional
    E) Devoted

An amateur can refer to someone who is either new in their field, or who does ineffective and sloppy work. Therefore, the correct answer is A. Answers B, D, and E can all be eliminated as antonyms of the word amateur.

19. Ford compares himself to a dramatic critic because

    A) He wants to confuse the reader by making an illogical comparison.
    B) He likes to keep up on all of the recent plays, and considers himself an expert.
    C) Both have the job of informing people.
    D) He thinks that dramatic critics are fascinating and aspires to be one.
    E) None of the above

Line 3 states that the dramatic critic warns the public about plays, and the Ford warns them about bad men. Therefore, both have the job of informing people. Answers B and D can be eliminated because dramatic critics are not referenced at any other point in the passage. Answer A can be eliminated because the passage is written in third person, meaning that Ford is an object in the passage, not the one presenting the information. This means he cannot be attempting to confuse the reader.

20. Based on the passage, how did Ford feel about going to London?

    A) Uncertain
    B) Excited
    C) Relieved
    D) Stolid
    E) Ebullient

The passage indicates that Ford initially opposed the appointment and felt inadequate. Therefore, options B, C, and E can be eliminated since they indicate that he was happy about the appointment. Option D can be eliminated because he objected rather than being simply indifferent. Therefore, the correct answer is option A.

PASSAGE

(1) Perry was the first to discover it. (2) I saw him fussing with the valves that regulate the air supply. (3) And at the same time I experienced difficulty in breathing. (4) My head felt dizzy—my limbs heavy.

(5) I saw Perry crumple in his seat. He gave himself a shake and sat erect again. (6) Then he turned toward me.

(7) "Good-bye, David," he said. (8) "I guess this is the end," and then he smiled and closed his eyes.

(9) "Good-bye, Perry, and good luck to you," I answered, smiling back at him. (10) But I fought off that awful lethargy.

At the Earth's Core
By Edgar Rice Burroughs
I- Toward the Eternal Fires

21. Based on the passage, the speaker and Perry are most likely

  A) Bitter enemies
  B) New acquaintances
  C) Strangers
  D) Doctors
  E) Old friends

The speaker and Perry interact amicably with one another, so the options A and C can be eliminated. Option D is irrelevant to the passage, and it is unlikely to be correct without any additional information regarding it having been presented. This leaves answers B and E. Because they are clearly in a distressing situation, and yet taking time to say good-bye to one another and smile, it is more likely that they are old friends than new acquaintances (otherwise they would probably ignore one another). Therefore E is the correct answer.

22. In line 7, Perry says good-bye because

  A) He is going to get more oxygen
  B) He is going to fuss with the valves some more
  C) He wants David to leave
  D) He believes they are both going to die
  E) None of the above

The phrase "I guess this is the end" accompanied by the descriptions of fuzziness and lethargy indicate that most likely the two are in a dangerous situation, and running out of oxygen. Therefore, the correct answer is D, he believes they are both going to die.

23. As used in line 10, the word lethargy most closely means

    A) Finesse
    B) Fatigue
    C) Discursiveness
    D) Hunger
    E) Vertigo

Because the speaker describes being dizzy, the passage indicates that he is running out of oxygen, and Perry is falling asleep, the most likely meaning of the word lethargy is fatigue.

PASSAGE

(1) In the works of Shakespeare, the most wonderful genius the world has ever known, there is the enormous number of 15,000 different words, but almost 10,000 of them are obsolete or meaningless today.

(2) Every person of intelligence should be able to use his mother tongue correctly. (3) It only requires a little pains, a little care, a little study to enable one to do so, and the recompense is great.

How to Speak and Write Correctly
By Joseph Devlin
Chapter I

24. As used in line 3, the word "pains" most closely means

    A) Suffering
    B) Anguish
    C) Effort
    D) Insight
    E) Celerity

The author of the passage is trying to convince people to take more care with their words because it is not very difficult. He is mitigating the effort involved. Therefore, answers A and B can be eliminated because they would indicate that study would be difficult. Rather, answer C is the most likely possibility.

25. The word recompense in line 3 could be replaced with the word

    A) Need
    B) Reprieve
    C) Effort
    D) Reward
    E) Malady

The author is advocating that greater care and study be given to language. Therefore, the most logical answer is D, reward.

26. Based on the passage, the speaker would consider grammatical errors to be

    A) Abhorrent
    B) Justified
    C) Intrepid
    D) Plausible
    E) Quaint

Abhorrent means repugnant or distasteful. Based on the author's staunch support of giving more care and study to language, this is the most logical answer.

PASSAGE

(1) It was a glorious day, a day of Egypt's blue and gold. (2) The sky was a wash of water color; the streets a flood of molten amber. (3) A little wind from the north rustled the acacias and blew in his bronzed face cool reminders of the widening Nile and dancing waves.

(4) He remembered a chap he knew, who had a sailing canoe–but no, he was going to get a costume for a fool ball!

(5) Disgustedly he turned into the very modern and official-looking residence that was the home of his friend, Andrew McLean, and the offices of that far-reaching institution, the Agricultural Bank.

(6) A white-robed, red-sashed and red-fezed houseboy led him across the tiled entrance into the long room where McLean was concluding a conference with two men.

(7) "Not the least trace," McLean was saying. (8) "We've questioned all our native agents–"

(9) Afterwards Ryder remembered that indefinite little pause. (10) If the two men had not lingered–if McLean had not remembered that he was an excavator–if chance had not brushed the scales with lightning wings–!

(11) "Ever hear of a chap called Delcassé, Paul Delcassé, a French excavator?" (12) McLean suddenly asked of him.

The Fortieth Door
By Mary Hastings Bradley
Chapter I

27. The word "acacias" in line 3 most likely refers to

   A) A plant
   B) A piece of furniture
   C) A type of sailboat
   D) A herd of animals
   E) A skirt

Line 3 refers to the wind "rustling" the acacias, making furniture or a herd of animals an unlikely meaning for the word. Therefore, options B and D can be eliminated. It is also unlikely that "acacias" refers to a skirt because no people are mentioned in the description. Based on the fact that the rest of the description refers to landscape features (and because it is more logical to describe plants rustling than sailboats) the correct answer is A.

28. Based on his description in lines 1-3, what does the speaker think of Egypt?

    A) That it is stifling and horrid
    B) That it is extravagant and unrestrained
    C) That the people are frivolous and callow
    D) That it is a beautiful and lovely place
    E) That it is beautiful, but not someplace he would like to go

Lines 1-3 paint a beautiful picture of the scenery in Egypt, and use words such as "gold," "bronzed," and "cool reminders" all of which lend to the fact that the author thinks positively about Egypt. This means that answers A, B, and C can all be eliminated. Answer E can be eliminated because the author is clearly enjoying the Egyptian scenery, and the reference to the Nile indicates that he is currently in Egypt. Therefore, the correct answer is D.

29. Based on the passage, McLean is likely a(n)

    A) Author
    B) Archaeologist
    C) Investigator
    D) Criminal
    E) Marshal

The fact that McLean lives in a beautiful and stately home, and is clearly a well-respected individual means that answer D can be eliminated. Answer B can be eliminated because the passage refers to the speaker, Ryder, as an "excavator," meaning he is the archaeologist. McLean asks him about Delcasse because of this fact, indicating that he is most likely not an excavator. In McLean's conversation with the other men, he indicates that he has spoken with all his "agents." Therefore, he is most likely some sort of investigator. The correct answer is C.

30. As it is used in line 6, the word conference would most correctly be replaced with

    A) Presentation
    B) Consultation
    C) Convention
    D) Session
    E) Meeting

Because there are only three men in the room, it wouldn't make sense to replace the word conference with either convention or session. Therefore, answers C and D can be eliminated. It is also unlikely that McLean is giving a presentation to the two men, because they seem to be conversing back and forth. Based on this fact, that they are few in number, and that it is in his home, the word conference would most accurately be replaced with meeting. Therefore, the correct answer is E.

31. Based on the passage, McLean most likely

    A) Expected the speaker and intended all along to ask him about Paul Delcasse.
    B) Did not actually want the speaker's opinion about Paul Delcasse - he was just being kind.
    C) Was surprised by the speaker's arrival, and didn't know what to say to him.
    D) Did not expect the speaker, but decided to ask him when he arrived because it was an area he had knowledge in.
    E) Has something to hide about his conference, and is trying to distract the speaker from the fact.

Ryder describes that it was only by chance that he encountered the two men, making it unlikely that McLean knew that he was coming. Therefore, answer A can be eliminated. It is also unlikely that McLean was at a loss for words, as indicated in option C, because he doesn't pause or stumble when he sees Ryder. Also, if McLean wished to distract Ryder from the meeting, or didn't care about his opinion, he would most likely not draw him into the conversation. Therefore, the correct answer is D.

32. Which of the following best describes how Ryder feels about attending the ball?

    A) Excited
    B) Frightened
    C) Pleased
    D) Conflicted
    E) Repulsed

Ryder thinks of the ball as a "fool ball," and the passage describes him as turning away "disgustedly." Based on this description he is clearly not excited to be going to the ball, and is more accurately repulsed by it. Therefore, the correct answer is E.

33. Which of the following best matches the meaning of the word indefinite in line 9?

    A) Official
    B) Confusing
    C) Angry
    D) Short
    E) Caustic

McLean does not seem to be angry or upset in any way, so options C and E can be eliminated. Also, it wouldn't make sense to describe the pause as official or confusing; rather, it seems to merely be a natural lull in the conversation. Based on this and the fact that it is coupled with the word little, the correct answer is D, short.

PASSAGE 1

Excerpt from a book about various games in the Native American culture.

(1) I approached them and found that the game they were playing at was what they called the game of platter. (2) This is the game to which the Indians are addicted above all others. (3) They sometimes lose their rest and in some degree their very senses at it. (4) They stake all they are worth, and several of them have been known to continue at it till they have stript themselves stark naked and lost all their movables in their cabin.

Indian Games
By Andrew McFarland Davis
Platter or Dice.

PASSAGE 2

Excerpt from a book giving a history of great Native American heroes and Chiefs.

(5) It was midwinter. (6) A large herd of buffalo was reported by the game scout. (7) The hunters gathered at daybreak prepared for the charge. (8) The old chief had his tried charger equipped with a soft, pillow-like Indian saddle and a lariat. (9) His old sinew-backed hickory bow was examined and strung, and a fine straight arrow with a steel head carefully selected for the test.

Indian Heroes and Great Chieftains
Charles A Eastman
Two Strike

34. Based on the information in passage 1, the game "platter" involves

    A) Swimming
    B) Dice
    C) Hunting
    D) Gambling
    E) Drinking

The passage does not give any information about how the game is actually played. However, it does say that "they stake all they are worth…" indicating that the game does involve gambling. Therefore, the correct answer is D.

35. In the first passage the Indians are portrayed as _____, whereas in the second passage they are portrayed as _____.

   A) Reckless, majestic
   B) Laconic, bloodthirsty
   C) Irrational, Inefficient
   D) Purposeful, imposing
   E) None of the above

The first passage describes the game of platter, and depicts the Indians as irresponsible in the way that they play the game. What's more, they are described as immoderate to the point of gambling away their very clothes. The second passage creates an awing and respectful view of the Indians as they embark on a hunt. Therefore, the most correct option is A, reckless and majestic.

36. Neither of the passages portrays the Indians as

   A) Regal
   B) Ferocious
   C) Irrational
   D) Reckless
   E) Heedless

The first passage portrays them as irrational, reckless, and heedless in their gambling. This eliminates answers C, D, and E as possibilities. The second passage portrays them as regal, imposing, and majestic. Therefore answer A can be eliminated. This means that the correct answer is B. In neither passage are the Indians portrayed as bloodthirsty savages.

37. As it is used in line 8, the word charger refers to

   A) An electronic battery
   B) A weapon
   C) A horse
   D) A general
   E) An orator

The charger is described as being equipped with a saddle; therefore, the most likely option is C, a horse.

38. Which of the following is a better description of passage 1 than passage 2?

    A) Narrative
    B) Informal
    C) Complimentary
    D) Formal
    E) Both A and B

The first passage portrays the Indians as reckless savages, and is given from a first-person (narrative) and informal point of view. The second passage is written in third person, and with much more formal and respectful language. It is also more complimentary and flattering to the Indians. Therefore, the correct answer is E.

PASSAGE 1

Spain maintained control of the Philippine Islands for more than three centuries and a half, during which period the tyranny, misconduct and abuses of the Friars and the Civil and Military Administration exhausted the patience of the natives and caused them to make a desperate effort to shake off the unbearable galling yoke on the 26th and 31st August, 1896, then commencing the revolution in the provinces of Manila and Cavite.

True version of the Philippine Revolution
By Don Emilio Aguinaldo y Famy
Chapter I. The Revolution of 1896

PASSAGE 2

The greater order which reigned in the Philippines after the advent of the Spaniards, and still more the commerce they opened with America and indirectly with Europe, had the effect of greatly increasing the Island trade, and of extending it beyond the Indies to the Persian Gulf. Manila was the great mart for the products of Eastern Asia, with which it loaded the galleons that, as early as 1565, sailed to and from New Spain and brought back silver as their principal return freight.

The Former Philippines thru Foreign Eyes
By FedorJagor et al
Chapter II

39. The word "principal" as it is used at the end of passage 2 means

    A) A head of a school
    B) Lead actor
    C) Primary
    D) A professed rule
    E) Obligation

The ships are described as being "loaded" with silver, and Manila is described as a great port. This means that silver is a common export. Although all of the options give a possible definition of the word principal (or principle), the most likely option based on the context is C, primary.

40. According to passage 1, the people of the Philippines were

    A) Oppressed
    B) Lavish
    C) Masochistic
    D) Infallible
    E) Obtuse

The passage states that the Spaniards maintained control of the people, and describes their actions as "tyrannous." This makes A the logical choice. Answer B can be eliminated because the people are desperate and burdened, meaning that they are likely poor, not lavish. Answer C can be eliminated because it is not a burden that they have chosen themselves. Answers D and E can be eliminated because the passage makes no reference to their intelligence.

41. According to passage 2, the people of the Philippines were

    A) Suppressed by the Spaniards
    B) Angered by the Spanish presence
    C) Harangued by the Spanish presence
    D) Enriched by the Spanish presence
    E) Befuddled by the Spanish presence

The second passage describes the fact that trade in the Philippines was uplifted and heightened under Spanish control. The answer choice which best describes this fact is answer D, that the people were enriched. Although answer A is a correct description of the first passage, it is not stated in the second passage.

42. Neither of the passages describes the Spaniards as

    A) Exploitive
    B) Tyrannical
    C) Mercantile
    D) Industrious
    E) Illusory

The first passage describes the Spanish as tyrannous, oppressive, and abusive. Therefore answers A and B can be eliminated. Answers C and D can be eliminated because the second passage describes the fact that the Spanish brought trade to the Islands, and improved their status in that way. Therefore, the correct answer is E, illusory.

43. The word "exhausted" as it is used in the middle of passage 1 means

   A) Fatigued
   B) Squandered
   C) Emptied
   D) Escaped
   E) Drained

Fatigued, emptied, and drained are all possible definition of the word exhausted, so options B and D can be eliminated because they are not. Answer A can be eliminated because it does not make a lot of sense to say that their patience has be "tired" because patience is not alive. Answer C can be eliminated because patience is not a physical object and therefore cannot be filled or emptied. Therefore, the correct answer is E.

44. Both passages indicate that

   A) Cavite was the first province to rebel against Spain.
   B) The Philippine Revolution lasted for 12 years.
   C) The Spanish were in control of the Philippines.
   D) Philippine trade was greatly improved by the Spanish presence.
   E) The Spaniards were oppressive towards the Philippine people.

Answers A and E are indicated in the first passage, but they are not in the second so this answer can be eliminated. Answer D is indicated in the second passage but not the first so this answer can be eliminated. Answer B is not indicated in either passage so this answer can be eliminated. Therefore, the correct answer is C.

45. Which Philippine province was the first to rebel?

   A) Manila
   B) Guimaras
   C) Antique
   D) Cavite
   E) Zambales

The only two provinces which are even mentioned in the passages are Manila and Cavite. Therefore, answers B, C, and E can be eliminated. The passage first lists two dates and then "Manila and Cavite." Based on parallelism, Manila will match up with the first date because it was listed first. Therefore, the correct answer is A.

46. Which of the passages was most likely written by a Philippine citizen?

   A) Passage 1 because it is more supportive of Philippine rights
   B) Passage 2 because it is less complimentary of the Spanish
   C) Passage 1 because it is more complimentary of the Spanish
   D) Both are equally likely to have been written by Philippine citizens
   E) Both are most likely written by Spaniards

The first passage is scathing towards the Spanish people, and supportive of the Philippine decision to rebel. However, the second passage is highly complementary of the Spanish. This makes it more likely that the first passage was written by a Philippine citizen. Therefore the correct answer is A.

PASSAGE 1

An excerpt from a Celtic fairytale

(1) Connla of the Fiery Hair was son of Conn of the Hundred Fights. (2) One day as he stood working by the side of his father on the height of Usna, he saw a maiden clad in strange attire coming towards him.
(3) "Whence comest thou, maiden?" said Connla.
(4) "I come from the Plains of the Ever Living," she said, "there where there is neither death nor sin. (5) There we keep holiday alway, nor need we help from any in our joy. (6) And in all our pleasure we have no strife. And because we have our homes in the round green hills, men call us the Hill Folk."

Celtic Fairy Tales
By Joseph Jacobs
Connla and the Fairy Maiden

PASSAGE 2

An excerpt from an English fairytale

(7) Once upon a time there was an old man, and an old woman, and a little boy. (8) One morning the old woman made a Johnny-cake, and put it in the oven to bake. (9) "You watch the Johnny-cake while your father and I go out to work in the garden." (10) So the old man and the old woman went out and began to hoe potatoes, and left the little boy to tend the oven. (11) But he didn't watch it all the time, and all of a sudden he heard a noise, and he looked up and the oven door popped open, and out of the oven jumped Johnny-cake, and went rolling along end over end, towards the open door of the house.

English Fairy Tales
By Joseph Jacobs
Johnny-Cake

47. Based on the information in the two passages, the Celtic culture

   A) Accepts a more destitute and transient lifestyle than the English culture.
   B) Considers children more capable of working than the English culture.
   C) Uses their fairytales for instruction and teaching more so than the English culture.
   D) Is more concerned with the accumulation of wealth than the English culture.
   E) Considers children less capable of working than the English culture.

Neither of the passages makes references to the financial situation of the characters involved, so answers A and D can be eliminated. In the first passage, the Celtic fairytale, the son is working alongside his father. However, in the second fairytale the son is left behind while the remainder of the family goes to work. Therefore, the most logical choice is answer B.

48. Which of the following indicates that the English culture is fonder of wordplay than the Celtic culture?

   A) The shortening of "always" to "alway" in line 5 of the first passage.
   B) The use of the word "plain" instead of "plane" in the first passage.
   C) That the oven door is described as "popping" open in the second passage.
   D) The use of the descriptive name "Hill Folk" in the first passage.
   E) The personification of the Johnny-cake as an actual boy in the second passage.

The fact that the second passage makes use of the term Johnny-cake, which is set up to be a baked good and later takes on the qualities of a real boy, indicates that the English culture is fond of wordplay. However, all of the language in the first passage is straightforward. Therefore, the correct answer is E.

49. Based on the beginning of the first passage, the Celtic culture considers _____ to be important.

   A) Progenitors
   B) Lineage
   C) Acuity
   D) Longevity
   E) Descendants

The first passage begins by indicating the lineage (family relations or ancestry) of the lead character. This indicates that lineage is an important aspect of the culture. Therefore, the correct answer is B.

50. The word "clad" as used in line 2 would best be replaced by the word

   A) Adorned
   B) Attacked
   C) Enveloped
   D) Unfettered
   E) Garbled

The maiden is described as being "clad in attire." Attire refers to clothing or what she is dressed in. The only word which fits in the context of clothing is adorned. Therefore, the correct answer is A.

51. Based on the information presented in the two passages, which of the following statements is TRUE?

   A) The English culture is more warlike and domineering than the Celtic culture.
   B) The Celtic culture is critical of a society in which there is no strife or work.
   C) Children in both cultures are considered useless and a drain on society.
   D) The Celtic culture idealizes a utopian society where this is no strife or work.
   E) The English culture is framed by bitterness about the gradual loss of rights to the monarchy.

Answer A can be eliminated because neither of the passages are about war or fighting, so it is irrational to draw this conclusion from them. Answer B can be eliminated because it is more likely that the culture is intrigued by such as society. This can be assumed both because it is true in a general sense, and the maiden from such a culture is described as beautiful and intrigues the lead character. Answer C can be eliminated because the son in the first passage is helping his father, not wasting time. Answer E can be eliminated because the passage does not mention political issues. Therefore, the correct answer is D.

52. The "Hill Folk" in the first passage can best be described as

   A) A war-torn land
   B) A utopian society
   C) A mythical people
   D) A totalitarian society
   E) None of the above

The Hill Folk's land seems to be a perfect place, with no work or war. Rather the people live in harmony and peace. This is what a utopian society is – a perfect place. Therefore, the correct answer is B.

PASSAGE

An excerpt from a biography of President Abraham Lincoln's life.

(1) Lincoln was a man of great sagacity. (2) Few statesmen have had keener insight, or more true and sane foresight. (3) While cordially recognizing this, it is not necessary to claim for him infallibility. (4) He had his disappointments.

The Life of Abraham Lincoln
By Henry Ketcham
Chapter XXVI. The War Here to Stay

53. Based on the passage, the author most likely considers Lincoln to be

  A) A bad President who just made mistakes.
  B) A decent man, but a terrible President.
  C) An imperfect man, but still highly admirable President.
  D) A detestable man, but an excellent President.
  E) A callow and naïve man when it comes to war.

The passage cites Lincoln as both sagacious and fallible. Therefore, the author believes him to have been a great man, but who was flawed by nature of being human. Therefore, the most correct option is C.

54. The word keener in line 2 could most correctly be replaced with the word

  A) Sharper
  B) Duller
  C) Stranger
  D) Darker
  E) Handsomer

The word keener is an adjective for intellect, or knowledge. Therefore, answers C, D, and E can be eliminated because they do not make sense in reference to knowledge. Because the passage is stating that Lincoln was a wise man, answer B can be eliminated because it would indicate that he was foolish. Therefore, the correct answer is A.

PASSAGE

(1) On the second day, at a distance of five hundred miles from the French coast, in the midst of a violent storm, we received the following message by means of the wireless telegraph:

(2) "Arsene Lupin is on your vessel, first cabin, blonde hair, wound right fore-arm, traveling alone under name of R........."

(3) At that moment, a terrible flash of lightning rent the stormy skies. (4) The electric waves were interrupted. (5) The remainder of the dispatch never reached us. (6) Of the name under Arsene Lupin was concealing himself, we knew only the initial.

(7) If the news had been of some other character, I have no doubt that the secret would have been carefully guarded by the telegraphic operator as well as by the officers of the vessel. (8) But it was one of those events calculated to escape from the most rigorous discretion. (9) The same day, no one knew how, the incident became a matter of current gossip and every passenger was aware that the famous Arsene Lupin was hiding in our midst.

(10) Arsene Lupin in our midst! (11) The irresponsible burglar whose exploits had been narrated in all the newspapers during the past few months! (12) The mysterious individual with whom Ganimard, our shrewdest detective, had been engaged in an implacable conflict amidst interesting and picturesque surroundings. (13) Arsene Lupin, the eccentric gentleman who operates only in the chateaux and salons, and who, one night, entered the residence of Baron Schormann, but emerged empty-handed, leaving, however, his card on which he had scribbled these words: "Arsene Lupin, gentleman-burglar, will return when the furniture is genuine." (14) Arsene Lupin, the man of a thousand disguises: in turn a chauffeur, detective, bookmaker, Russian physician, Spanish bull-fighter, commercial traveler, robust youth, or decrepit old man.

The Extraordinary Adventures of Arsene Lupin, Gentleman Burglar
By Maurice Leblanc
I. The Arrest of Arsene Lupin

55. Based on the information in the passage, the people are traveling by

    A) Car
    B) Hot air balloon
    C) Plane
    D) Ship
    E) Submarine

The first line describes their location in reference to the French coast, which makes it most probable that the people are traveling by something in the water. Also, the passage indicates that there are quite a few passengers (enough that they do not all know each other) and that they are on board for a number of days. Furthermore, line 7 refers to them being on a "vessel" which is a term used to describe ships. Therefore, the correct answer is D.

56. The word "the incident" in line 9 is referring to

    A) The storm
    B) The telegraph
    C) The injury of Arsene Lupin
    D) The night's dinner
    E) None of the above

The passage does not go into much detail about Lupin's injury, and does not ever mention dinner. Furthermore, after the passage mentions the incident, it begins to discuss the gossip about Arsene Lupin, whose presence was learned of via the telegraph. Therefore, it is referring to the telegraph and the correct answer is B.

57. Based on the description in line 14, Arsene Lupin could be described as a

    A) Tiger
    B) Dog
    C) Snake
    D) Snail
    E) Chameleon

Arsene Lupin is described as being a master at disguising himself. He takes on many different disguises to pull off his stunts and is never recognized. Despite his fame, none of the passengers on the ship are even sure who he is. Therefore, he is most like a chameleon because they can camouflage themselves to hide in plain sight.

58. The speaker of the passage seems to feel how about Arsene Lupin?

    A) Fascinated
    B) Conciliatory
    C) Disputing
    D) Critical
    E) Effusive

The speaker seems excited when he begins describing the many impressive feats of Arsene Lupin. He describes him as though he is a celebrity and not a criminal. If he were critical or disputing towards him then he would likely not describe him in such favorable or admiring terms. Therefore, the correct answer is A.

59. The word "implacable" in line 12 means

    A) Slow
    B) Relentless
    C) Ruthless
    D) Unwitting
    E) Ebullient

The word implacable is used to describe the detective's tireless efforts to track down Arsene Lupin for many months. This fact is best described by answer B, relentless.

60. The speaker of the passage is of what nationality?

    A) Sicilian
    B) Spanish
    C) French
    D) English
    E) American

The passage begins by noting the ship's distance from the French coast, so it is likely that the speaker has some connection to France. As the passage continues, the speaker shows his great knowledge of a French criminal's actions. Furthermore, in describing the French detective he calls him "our shrewdest detective" indicating that he is, in fact, French himself.

61. "Engaged" as used in line 12 means

   A) Promised to be married
   B) Involved
   C) Secured
   D) Betrothed
   E) Discharged

Although all of the answers are possible interpretations of the word engaged, the detective is not "promised to be married" to Arsene Lupin. Rather, he is trying to track him down. Therefore, answers A, C, and D can be eliminated. Answer E can be eliminated because the detective has been hired to find Lupin, not discharged from this duty. Therefore, the correct answer is B.

62. Based on line 13, Arsene Lupin can best be described as a

   A) White-collar criminal
   B) Corporate criminal
   C) War criminal
   D) Blue-collar criminal
   E) National hero

Answer E can be eliminated because Arsene Lupin is quite clearly a thief, not a national hero. Answer D can be eliminated because Arsene Lupin is described as being a clever and precise thief, not a man who works by violence. The term white-collar criminal best describes Lupin because he is described as a "gentleman-burglar" and only deals with high-value collector items that will get a lot of attention. Therefore, the correct answer is A.

PASSAGE 1

(1) Unlike actual law, Internet software has no capacity to punish. (2) It doesn't affect people who aren't online (and only a tiny minority of the world population is). (3) And if you don't like the Internet's system, you can always flip off the modem.

Free Culture
By Lawrence Lessig (Quoting David Pogue)
Preface

PASSAGE 2

(4) This rough divide between the free and the controlled has now been erased. (5) The Internet has set the stage for this … (6) The technology that preserved the balance of our history—between uses of our culture that were free and uses of our culture that were only upon permission—has been undone. (7) The consequence is that we are less and less a free culture, more and more a permission culture.

Free Culture
By Lawrence Lessig
Introduction

63. As used in line 1 of the first passage, the word "capacity" means

    A) Competence
    B) Available area
    C) Occupation
    D) Ability
    E) Mental acuity

The passage is describing the fact that the internet is not able to affect people who aren't online. This description is best embodied by answer D, ability.

64. The first passage regards the internet as _____, whereas the second passage regards it as _____.

    A) Irrelevant, Harmful
    B) Useful, Immaterial
    C) Useless, Enigmatic
    D) Ponderous, Destructive
    E) Inspiring, Execrable

The first passage indicates that the internet cannot affect people, and is really not an important factor in most people's lives. This description fits only options A and C (irrelevant and useless), so options B, D, and E can be eliminated. The second passage describes the fact that the internet is bringing an end to free culture. Therefore, the correct answer is A.

65. What is meant by the term "permission culture" used in line 7 of the second passage?

    A) A culture where individuals have to please everyone
    B) A culture that is not controlled at all
    C) A culture where people can say what they want
    D) A culture where people have to get permission to do things
    E) A culture that is subject to regulations

The passage is describing the fact that people can only post things on the internet if the government allows them, which has changed the ability of culture to spread. This means that answers B and C can be eliminated. Rather, it describes the fact that the internet is regulated. Therefore, answer E is the correct answer.

66. The author of passage 2 would most likely disagree with which statement?

    A) The internet has made a great impact on culture
    B) The internet has hindered the spread of culture
    C) The internet can only affect those who are connected to it
    D) The internet has destroyed the free spread of culture
    E) All of the above

Passage 2 argues that world culture as a whole, which affects everyone, has been changed by the internet. Therefore, the author of passage 2 believes that the internet affects everyone. This means that the author of passage 2 would most likely disagree with statement C.

67. The author of passage 1 would most likely disagree with which statement?

    A) The internet is not widespread enough to impact most people
    B) The internet has changed the way that world culture spreads
    C) The internet's effects can be avoided
    D) Most people do not use the internet
    E) None of the above

Passage 1 argues that the internet is essentially irrelevant to most of the world because most of the world cannot actually access it. This means that answers A, C, and D can all be eliminated because they are in line with this belief. Answer B, however, more accurately describes the belief of the author of passage 1, not passage 2. Therefore, the correct answer is B.

68. Neither of the passages

    A) Considers the internet irrelevant
    B) States that the internet has ended free culture
    C) Notes the impact of the internet on world culture
    D) Considers the internet to be regulated
    E) Advocates the internet

Passage 1 describes answer A, therefore this can be eliminated. Passage 2 does answers B, C, and D so they can be eliminated. Passage 1 takes the stand that the internet is irrelevant, and passage 2 takes the stand that it is harmful. Therefore, neither passage advocates the use of the internet, and answer E is the correct answer.

PASSAGE

(1) Since they are so frequently encountering goodness, both laymen and scholars are apt to assume that it is altogether clear and requires no explanation. (2) But the very reverse is the truth. (3) Familiarity obscures. It breeds instincts and not understanding. (4) So inwoven has goodness become with the very web of life that it is hard to disentangle.

The Nature of Goodness
By George Herbert Palmer
I. The Double Aspect of Goodness

69. Line 2

    A) Reinforces line 1
    B) Enhances line 1
    C) Negates line 4
    D) Negates line 1
    E) Reinforces line 4

Line 2 states that line 1 is completely wrong. Therefore it negates, or undoes, line 1. This makes option D the correct answer.

70. "Obscures" in line 3 means

    A) Faints
    B) Conceals
    C) Illuminates
    D) Clarifies
    E) Distinguishes

The definition of the word obscures is to hide or conceal or make difficult to understand or see. Therefore, the correct answer is option B.

71. The author of the passage would most likely agree with which statement?

    A) Defining the origin of goodness dates back centuries and is quite intricate.
    B) Goodness is an abstract concept that is actually quite difficult to define.
    C) In today's society, it is very rare for truly good things to happen to people.
    D) People are very adept at recognizing good things when they happen.
    E) None of the above

Answer D can be eliminated because the passage states that people who see good are the worst at understanding or identifying it. Rather, the passage argues that goodness is difficult to understand. Therefore, answer B is the correct option.

PASSAGE

Jimmie Dale, a well-known gentlemen, has just returned from breaking into a house on West Broadway

(1) Again the telephone rang insistently. (2) He reached languidly for the receiver, took it off its hook, and held it to his ear.
(3) "Hello!" said Jimmie Dale, with a sleepy yawn. (4) "Hello! Hello! Why the deuce don't you yank a man out of bed at two o'clock in the morning and have done with it, and–eh? (5) Oh, that you, Carruthers?"
(6) "Yes," came Carruthers' voice excitedly. (7) "Jimmie, listen–listen! (8) The Gray Seal's come to life! (9) He's just pulled a break on West Broadway!"
(10) "Good Lord!" gasped Jimmie Dale. (11) "You don't say!"

The Adventures of Jimmie Dale I
By Frank L Packard
Part One: The Man in the Case – Chapter I: The Gray Seal

72. The word "languidly" in line 2 would most correctly be replaced by

  A) Lazily
  B) Excitedly
  C) Ebulliently
  D) Laboriously
  E) Rancorously

Languidly means tiredly or lethargically. Furthermore, Jimmie dale is later described as sleepy, and the passage indicates that it is the middle of the night. Therefore "lazily" would be the most correct choice to replace languidly, and the correct answer is A.

73. The phrase "you don't say" in line 11 is meant to indicate that

  A) Jimmie Dale is upset by the information
  B) Jimmie Dale does not want Carruthers to say what he did
  C) Jimmie Dale think that Carruthers is overstepping his bounds
  D) Jimmie Dale wants Carruthers to repeat what he has said
  E) Jimmie Dale is surprised by the information

Carruthers believes that he has just revealed some interesting information, and Jimmie Dale is described as gasping when he hears it. Therefore, the most likely option is that it is meant to indicate that he is surprised by what has been said.

74. Based on the information provided in the passage, Jimmie Dale is

   A) Carruthers' brother
   B) The mayor
   C) The Gray Seal
   D) A manservant
   E) None of the above

The summary before the passage indicates that Jimmie Dale has just robbed a house in the same location that Carruthers states that the Gray Seal was just seen. This makes it most likely that Jimmie Dale is secretly the Gray Seal.

75. The "Gray Seal" is most likely

   A) A popular attraction at the local zoo
   B) A precision burglar
   C) A statue of a seal on West Broadway
   D) A code word between the two friends
   E) A novel that Carruthers has been writing

Line 9 indicates that the Gray Seal is some sort of robber who has just been seen. Therefore, the correct answer is option B.

PASSAGE 1

(1) Although some feeling for beauty is perhaps universal among men, the same cannot be said of the understanding of beauty. (2) The average man, who may exercise considerable taste in personal adornment, in the decoration of the home, or in the choice of poetry and painting, is at a loss when called upon to tell what art is or to explain why he calls one thing "beautiful" and another "ugly."

The Principles of Aesthetics
By Dewitt H. Parker
Chapter I – Introduction: Purpose and Method

PASSAGE 2

(3) In aesthetic criticism the first step towards seeing one's object as it really is, is to know one's own impression as it really is, to discriminate it, to realise it distinctly. (4) The objects with which aesthetic criticism deals… possess, like the products of nature, so many virtues or qualities. (5) …And he who experiences these impressions strongly, and drives directly at the discrimination and analysis of them, has no need to trouble himself with the abstract question what beauty is in itself.

The Renaissance: Studies in Art and Poetry
By Walter Pater
Preface

76. According to passage 1, the understanding of beauty is

    A) Finite and not subject to personal opinions
    B) Abstract and difficult for many people to grasp
    C) Ethereal and easy to confuse with aesthetics
    D) Universal and easy to communicate
    E) All of the above

The first passage states that the average person "is at a loss when called upon to tell what art is." This indicates that beauty is difficult to understand. Therefore, the correct answer is option B.

77. According to passage 2, the understanding of beauty

A) Is finite and not subject to personal opinion
B) Is a universal truth and everyone should be in agreement
C) Is abstract and difficult for most people to consider for themselves
D) Begins by assessing personal opinions
E) None of the above

The second passage states that "the first step towards seeing one's object as it really is, is to know one's own impression as it really is." Therefore, answer D is a correct statement. Based on this fact, answer C can be eliminated because it argues that people cannot have personal options about beauty. Answers B and A also imply that personal opinions are not relevant to considering beauty. Therefore, the correct answer is D.

78. The word "exercise" as used in line 2 means

A) Work out
B) Train
C) Compose
D) Activity
E) Apply

Although answers A, B, and C are all possible interpretations of the word exercise, the passages are both about art and none of these options makes sense in this context. Answer C is not a meaning of the word exercise so it can also be eliminated. Therefore, the correct answer is option E.

79. The word "discriminate" used in line 3 could most correctly be replaced with

A) Define
B) Judge
C) Favor
D) Criticize
E) Dislike

Line 3 is indicating that a person must identify and understand their own opinions about beauty. Therefore, the most correct answer is option A, define, because it is most similar to this meaning.

80. Both passages agree that

    A) It is not possible for people to experience beauty because it is so abstract.
    B) All people have the same opinion about what is beautiful.
    C) Beauty is abstract and, to a certain extent, personal.
    D) People should all write novels about their personal impressions of beauty.
    E) Sculpture is the most beautiful art medium, and the easiest to study.

Answer A can be eliminated because passage one indicates that despite the fact that people cannot adequately describe or explain beauty, everyone can recognize it. Answer B can be eliminated because both passages indicate that people have personal opinions about beauty. Therefore, answer C is correct because it states this fact. Answers D and E can be eliminated because the passages do not refer to them at all.

81. The author of which passage would most likely agree with the statement that a specific definition of beauty is irrelevant?

    A) Passage 1 because the passage states that "the average man" does not know how to define beauty.
    B) Passage 2 because the passage states that impressions if beauty are more important than explanations of beauty.
    C) Passage 2 because the passage states that aesthetic criticism is the most important type of criticism that there is.
    D) Neither author is likely to agree with this.
    E) Both authors would most likely agree with this.

Passage 2 indicates that it is important for people to understand their own opinions and impressions about beauty. Therefore, answer B is correct.

PASSAGE

(1) When I finished school I was as raw as raw could be.... (2) So I started out by helping at an aquarium shop in Mapusa, the town nearest my village. (3) The proprietor of the shop is Ashok D'Cruz.... (4) I accompanied Ashok to a client's office to put a pair of Dwarf Guramies in the fish tank and to fix a picture as a backdrop for the tank. (5) On such visits I watched carefully what Ashok did and soon enough Ashok started sending me on my own to visit some of his clients who had small or simple problems.

Free from School
By Rahul Alvares
Chapter 1: A Fish Shop in Mapusa

82. The word "raw" in line 1 can be interpreted to mean

   A) Confident
   B) Stupid
   C) Genius
   D) Inexperienced
   E) Undercooked

The speaker has just finished his schooling, so he is likely not stupid. Answer E can be eliminated because it would be illogical to describe a person as undercooked. The fact that the speaker takes a small job working in an aquarium indicates that he does not have a lot of experience, making answer D the most correct choice.

83. The speaker can best be described as a(n)

   A) Apprentice
   B) Entrepreneur
   C) Student
   D) Father
   E) Teacher

The speaker has just finished schooling, so he is likely not a father and he is no longer a student. He works at a local shop, so he cannot be an entrepreneur or a teacher. Therefore, the correct option is A. This is logical because he is working for another person and learning a craft from them.

84. The "Dwarf Guarmies" mentioned in line 4 are most likely

    A) Pictures
    B) Trinkets
    C) Fish
    D) Machinery
    E) Mythical creatures

The speaker works in an aquarium, and is helping work on a fish tank. Therefore, they are most likely a type of fish that the tank owner wished to purchase.

PASSAGE

(1) Human isolation is an unnatural condition. (2) It antagonizes the highest and best interests of the world. (3) Its influence is never beneficent, but always and necessarily harmful. (4) If the truest well-being of the universe, and the supremest glory of Jehovah could have been attained by conditions of solitude, it is not impossible that the good All-Father would have given to every man a continent, and so have made him monarch of all he surveyed.

The Jericho Road
By W. Biom Adkins
Early Organizations.

85. The author of this passage would most agree with which statement?

  A) There is no need for kings and rulers
  B) People are meant to be alone
  C) The "good All-Father" is wrong
  D) Marriage is an unholy institution
  E) People are not meant to be alone

The passage is a statement that being alone is bad for humans, and that humans were not created to live in isolation. Therefore, the author of the passage would most likely agree with statement E.

86. The word "its" at the beginning of line 3 refers to

  A) "the world" (line 2)
  B) "human isolation" (line 1)
  C) "an unnatural condition" (line 1)
  D) "Jehovah" (line 4)
  E) "the good All-Father" (line 4)

The passage is all about how being alone is not good for people, and that people were not meant to live in isolation. The "its" in line 3 is described as a harmful influence. Therefore, "its" is referring to human isolation from line 1, and is describing it further.

87. The most correct interpretation of the word "surveyed" at the end of line 4 is

    A) Oversaw
    B) Reviewed
    C) Polled
    D) Examined
    E) Conversed

The word surveyed is used to describe all that the person is in control of, and the land that they occupy. Therefore, the most logical interpretation of surveyed is answer A, oversaw. Options B, C, E and E can be eliminated because it would not make sense in the context of the line to do these actions to a stretch of land.

PASSAGE

(1) If, when I was a boy, and went forth into the world poor and friendless, a good fairy had met me and said, (2) "Choose now thy own course through life, and the object for which thou wilt strive, and then, according to the development of thy mind, and as reason requires, I will guide and defend thee to its attainment," (3) my fate could not, even then, have been directed more happily, more prudently, or better.

The True Story of My Life
By Hans Christian Andersen
Chapter I.

88. Based on the passage, the author feels that his life

    A) Never went how he wanted
    B) Was quite happy
    C) Didn't meet his childhood expectations
    D) Could not have been worse
    E) Was too controlled

In line 3 the speaker states that he could not have had a better life if he had chosen it himself. Therefore, answer B is the correct answer.

89. The word "object" in line 2 would most correctly be replaced by the word

    A) Item
    B) Article
    C) Goal
    D) Subject
    E) None of the above

Because the overall tone of the passage is concentrated on the positive summary of a life, it stands to reason that this would be a goal, answer choice C.

PASSAGE

(1) Soon after I had thus gained a complete victory over my two powerful adversaries, my companion arrived in search of me; for finding I did not follow him into the wood, he returned, apprehending I had lost my way, or met with some accident.

(2) After mutual congratulations, we measured the crocodile, which was just forty feet in length.

(3) As soon as we had related this extraordinary adventure to the governor, he sent a wagon and servants, who brought home the two carcasses. (4) The lion's skin was properly preserved, with its hair on, after which it was made into tobacco-pouches, and presented by me, upon our return to Holland, to the burgomasters, who, in return, requested my acceptance of a thousand ducats.

(5) The skin of the crocodile was stuffed in the usual manner, and makes a capital article in their public museum at Amsterdam, where the exhibitor relates the whole story to each spectator, with such additions as he thinks proper...

(6) The little regard which this impudent knave has to veracity makes me sometimes apprehensive that my real facts may fall under suspicion, by being found in company with his confounded inventions.

The Adventures of Baron Munchausen
By Rudolph Enrich Raspe
Chapter 1

90. The two powerful adversaries referenced in line 1 are

    A) Two poachers who the speaker stopped in the act of poaching
    B) Two friends with whom the speaker was involved in a game of bridge
    C) A lion and a crocodile
    D) Two lions that the speaker had been hunting all day
    E) Two crocodiles who had attacked the speaker as he stopped for a rest

The passage continues on after line 1 to describe how the speaker and his friend treat a lion and a crocodile which the speaker has obtained. Therefore, it is most likely that these are the adversaries that it is referencing.

91. How does the speaker feel about the museum exhibitor?

    A) He dislikes him because he makes the story sound less impressive
    B) He thinks he is an excellent exhibitor because he is truthful
    C) He dislikes him because he refuses to display the crocodile
    D) He appreciates his skill in telling a story
    E) He dislikes him because he is not always truthful in his presentations

In line 6 the exhibitor is described as an "impudent knave," which is an insulting description and indicates that the speaker of the passage does not like the exhibitor. Furthermore, he describes him as untruthful. This means that answer E is correct.

92. As used in line 1, the word "apprehending" means

    A) Understanding
    B) Worrying
    C) Excited
    D) Unconcerned that
    E) Accepting

The speaker has just engaged in a battle with a lion and a tiger, and is clearly in a dangerous location. The fact that the companion begins a worried search when he discovers the speaker missing further indicates this fact. Therefore, the most probable interpretation is B, worrying.

93. Based on the treatment that the speaker receives in lines 3-5, his actions

    A) Were illegal, and everyone is setting him up to be arrested
    B) Were quite impressive, and everyone is surprised by his abilities
    C) Were fairly mundane, and people are not particularly concerned with them
    D) Were exactly what was expected, and of little note
    E) None of the above

In lines 3-5 the speaker is praised for his actions, and his catches are placed on display in museums. This indicates that what he did was impressive. This is best described by answer B.

94. Based on line 1

   A) It was the speaker's intention all along face the two adversaries
   B) It was the guide's intention that the speaker face the two adversaries
   C) It was chance and necessity that resulted in the speaker facing the two adversaries
   D) The two adversaries hunted down the speaker to confront him
   E) The two adversaries were avoiding the speaker, but he confronted them anyways

The guide was surprised to find the speaker missing, so option B can be eliminated. Option A can be eliminated because if the companion was surprised to have lost track of him, it is not likely that the speaker intended to hunt the adversaries. Answers D and E can be eliminated because it is unlikely that a lion and a crocodile were hunting down the speaker. Therefore, the correct answer is C.

95. Based on line 6, the actual manner in which the speaker overcame the two adversaries is

   A) Far-fetched and fantastic
   B) Boring and mundane
   C) Modest and typical
   D) Noteworthy and reprehensible
   E) None of the above

Answer D can be eliminated because it is illogical to describe anything as both noteworthy (impressive) and reprehensible (shameful). Answers C and B can be eliminated because the speaker would not have received such praise if his actions were typical or boring. The speaker is worried that people will not believe the real story of what happened, so answer A is the most likely option.

96. The word "capital" as used in line 6 means

    A) Uppercase
    B) Metropolis
    C) Distinct
    D) Monetary
    E) Excellent

The word capital is being used to describe the display. This means that answers A-D can be eliminated because none of them would be used to describe a display. Therefore, the correct answer is E, excellent.

97. The "confounded inventions" referred to in line 6 are

    A) The untruthful stories that the exhibitor tells about the display
    B) Gadgets the exhibitor uses to clean displays
    C) False displays which the exhibitor uses to impress tourists
    D) Animatronic lions which the exhibitor uses in his presentations
    E) None of the above

It is the exhibitor's job to tell people about the different displays. The speaker is worried that he will exaggerate and tell different stories about the display. Therefore, the correct answer is option A because it describes this fact.

98. Based on line 1, the speaker is in a location that is

    A) Well-explored
    B) Safe
    C) Monitored by cameras
    D) Dangerous
    E) Languid

The speaker describes that he has just encountered adversaries, and that his companion is worried to find him missing. Therefore, the location is most likely not particularly safe. Therefore, the correct answer is option D.

PASSAGE

(1) "You gave me more uneasiness than any child I had," his mother once said to [John], in her old age.
(2) "I suppose you were afraid I wouldn't live," he suggested.
(3) She looked at him with the keen humor which had been her legacy to him. (4) "No, afraid you would," she said. (5) Which was only her joke, for she had the tenderest of hearts, and, like all mothers, had a weakness for the child that demanded most of her mother's care.

99. The word "legacy" in line 3 means

   A) Payment
   B) Gift
   C) Fear
   D) Inheritance
   E) Complaint

A legacy is something that is passed on from generation to generation. This is best described by the word "inheritance. Therefore, the correct answer is D.

100. Based on the passage, the mother

   A) Has a great affection for her son
   B) Does not like her son very much
   C) Considers her son to have been more trouble than he was worth
   D) Wishes that her son had better life prospects
   E) Wishes her son had not lived through his childhood

Although the mother indicates that she was afraid her son would live, the passage makes it clear that this is a joke. Furthermore, the passage indicates that the mother is tender-hearted, and has a weakness for her son. Therefore, the correct answer is A.

Passages Answer Key

1. E	39. C	77. D
2. C	40. A	78. E
3. B	41. D	79. A
4. C	42. E	80. C
5. C	43. E	81. B
6. A	44. C	82. D
7. D	45. A	83. A
8. D	46. A	84. C
9. B	47. B	85. E
10. E	48. E	86. B
11. D	49. B	87. A
12. C	50. A	88. B
13. A	51. D	89. C
14. D	52. B	90. C
15. E	53. C	91. E
16. C	54. A	92. B
17. B	55. D	93. B
18. A	56. B	94. C
19. C	57. E	95. A
20. A	58. A	96. E
21. E	59. B	97. A
22. D	60. C	98. D
23. B	61. B	99. D
24. C	62. A	100. A
25. D	63. D	
26. A	64. A	
27. A	65. E	
28. D	66. C	
29. C	67. B	
30. E	68. E	
31. D	69. D	
32. E	70. B	
33. D	71. B	
34. D	72. A	
35. A	73. E	
36. B	74. C	
37. C	75. B	
38. E	76. B	

Test Taking Strategies

Here are some test-taking strategies that are specific to this test and to other tests in general:

- Keep your eyes on the time. Pay attention to how much time you have left to complete that section.
- Read the entire question and read all the answers. Many questions are not as hard to answer as they may seem.
- Read the wording carefully. Some words can give you hints to the right answer. There are no exceptions to an answer when there are words in the question such as always, all or none. If one of the answer choices includes most or some of the right answers, but not all, then that is not the answer. Here is an example:

  The primary colors include all of the following:
  A) Red, Yellow, Blue, Green
  B) Red, Green, Yellow
  C) Red, Orange, Yellow
  D) Red, Yellow, Blue
  E) None of the above

  Although item A includes all the right answers, it also includes an incorrect answer, making it incorrect. If you didn't read it carefully, were in a hurry, or didn't know the material well, you might fall for this.

- Make a guess on a question that you do not know the answer to. There is no penalty for an incorrect answer. Eliminate the answer choices that you know are incorrect. For example, this could let your guess be a 1 in 3 chance at the correct answer.

What Your Score Means

You are scored from 200-800 in each subject area, reading, math and writing. Your scores from each section are added together resulting in a range from 600-2400. A score of 2400 is considered a perfect score. This study guide is a great way to increase your overall score. If you are ready to focus on a specific area and boost your score, this is the way to do it. Study and practice is really the only way to increase your score.

What is an average score? In 2011, the average scores were: 497 critical reading, 514 math, and 489 writing. Using round numbers, that's about 500 for each subject, about 1500 overall. How does that compare for your Ivy League and local schools?

College	SAT Critical Reading	SAT Mathematics	SAT Writing
Brown University	660-760	670-770	670-770
Harvard University	670-770	680-780	670-780
Texas A&M – College Station	530-650	570-680	510-620
UCLA	570-680	610-740	580-710
Yale University	700-800	700-780	700-790

Don't forget, for admissions, schools look at more than just your SAT scores – but having a great one helps! They look at GPA, courses taken (AP, dual-enrollment, honors), personal essay, meaningful service, school activities and school involvement.

Test Preparation

This book is much different than the regular SAT study guides. This book actually specifically focuses on an area to boost your scores as high as possible. It teaches you the information that you need to know to improve your score.

We use test questions to test your knowledge and to teach new information. If you don't know the answer to the test question, review the material. This is the best way to target your study to cover the information that you specifically need to know.

To prepare for the test, make a series of goals. Register and plan for the upcoming test. Then decide how much time each day you will schedule to review the information you have already studied and to learn additional material. Take notes as you study; it will help you learn the material. If you haven't done so already, download the study tips guide from the website and use it to start your study plan.

Legal Note

www.ingramcontent.com/pod-product-compliance
Lightning Source LLC
Chambersburg PA
CBHW050351100426
42739CB00015BB/3364